Albert J. Holden

Songs of Faith, Hope and Love

for Sunday schools and devotional meetings

Albert J. Holden

Songs of Faith, Hope and Love
for Sunday schools and devotional meetings

ISBN/EAN: 9783337090708

Printed in Europe, USA, Canada, Australia, Japan

Cover: Foto ©Lupo / pixelio.de

More available books at **www.hansebooks.com**

SONGS OF
FAITH, HOPE, AND LOVE.

"AND NOW ABIDETH FAITH, HOPE, LOVE; THESE THREE."

FOR

SUNDAY SCHOOLS

AND

DEVOTIONAL MEETINGS.

Compiled by

ALBERT J. HOLDEN.

NEW YORK:
WILLIAM A. POND & CO.,
25 UNION SQUARE.

CHICAGO:
CHICAGO MUSIC CO., 152 STATE ST.

INTRODUCTORY.

Among the many helpful aids to better work in the Sunday-school, nothing is so much needed as a good collection of hymns: hymns which shall be earnest, stirring, useful, and fairly meet the test of literary criticism. The larger part of the popular Sunday-school hymnology is open to grave censure for many serious literary defects; barren doggerel rhymes, strained metaphors, unhealthy sentiments, are bad enough, but coupled with these is a trite, familiar use of sacred epithets, and the appellations of the Deity and the Saviour, which are as offensive to correct taste as is the general illiteracy which is so marked a feature of the host of Sunday-school singing books whose titles are almost as numerous as the mineral and floral products from which they are named.

The best which could be said for the greater part of the music associated with these so-called hymns, was, that it was quickly and easily caught up: but time tests all things, and the little, jingling, superficial tunes were as quickly and easily dropped and forgotten, and the usefulness of the book was exhausted within two years at most.

Hymns and music, if good, have this quality in common with truth,—they abide and endure: if on the other hand, they are hollow, false, superficial, they, like all error, will pass away.

SONGS OF FAITH, HOPE, AND LOVE
is an earnest effort at improvement in the place it seeks to occupy. A hymn, properly considered, is an expression of praise, an act of devotion, not a statement of creed or dogma; and sectarian theology will fail to find a hymn in this collection which can be claimed as its peculiar property; at the same time there is not a line or sentiment in the entire book which cannot be heartily approved by Christians of every denomination. The title of this book is no random choice; every hymn in it is what a hymn should be,—*a song of faith, hope, and love.*

The music, if good and true, will find friends without a word being said in its behalf: to those, however, who think that any departure from the simplest harmony is inadmissible in Sunday-school music, it might be well to say that the many years experience of the compiler of this book has proven the fallacy of that idea, and shown conclusively that if the melody of a song be clearly and sharply defined, children will readily sing it without being misled by even more elaborate harmonies than any used in these pages.

Suitable hymns have been provided for the various festivals and occasions of special service, such as Christmas, Easter, the New Year, Anniversaries, National Holidays, Thanksgiving; and for such as may find it useful, a form of service with appropriate scriptural and musical selections for the opening exercises of a school will be found on the last pages. A number of standard hymns, with the names of familiar tunes attached, have been scattered through the book, and will be found serviceable at devotional meetings.

ACKNOWLEDGEMENT is due in this place, to many kind friends and sympathetic well-wishers, whose helpful labor in verse and song has added so much of strength and beauty to the value of this book: very many of its pages bear friendly evidence either of poet or musician who, with generous promptness responded to my wish for their best efforts.

Gratitude is also due to many unknown friends whose exquisite verses I have sometimes gleaned from various periodical publications, often with no name of author attached; should this book, haply, fall into the hands of any such, I shall be glad to further express my obligation.

More than two years of happy labor have been given to the preparation of this work; may that happiness be increased an hundred-fold to all who sing, whether from these or other pages, the Divine songs of faith, hope, and love.

ALBERT J. HOLDEN.

New York, New Year's Day, 1883.

TO

MRS. C. M. SAWYER,
COLLEGE HILL, MASS.,

THIS BOOK IS DEDICATED, WITH THE AFFECTIONATE REGARD
OF ONE OF HER SUNDAY SCHOOL SCHOLARS,

ALBERT J. HOLDEN.

SONGS OF FAITH, HOPE, AND LOVE.

THE ANGELS OF BETHLEHEM.

8 HARK! THE HOSTS OF HEAVEN ARE SINGING.

E. H. Plumptre.   CHRISTMAS HYMN.   German Melody.

1 { Hark! the hosts of heaven are sing-ing Prais-es to their
   Strains of sweet-est mu-sic fling-ing, Not a note or
new-born Lord. }
word un-heard. } This the day of days most ho-ly,
Day in which new joys were given Not in part, a-lone, but whol-ly, To the wide world un-der heaven.

2 On this night, all nights excelling,
   God's high praises sounded forth,
While the angels' songs were telling
   Of the Lord's mysterious Birth:
Through the darkness, strangely splendid
   Flashed the light on shepherds' eyes;
As their lowly flocks they tended,
   Came new tidings from the skies.

3 On this day then through creation
   Let the glorious hymn ring out;
Let men hail the great salvation,
   "God with us," with song and shout,
See, the powers of hell are broken,
   Fierce and tyrannous and wild;
And on earth glad words are spoken,
   Heralding the new born Child.

DEDHAM. (Key A.)

1 CALM on the listening ear of night,
    Come heaven's melodious strains,
    Where wild Judea stretches far
    Her silver-mantled plains.

2 The answering hills of Palestine
    Send back the glad reply;
    And greet, from all their holy heights,
    The dayspring from on high..

3 O'er the blue depths of Galilee
    There comes a holier calm,
    And Sharon waves, in solemn praise,
    Her silent groves of palm.

4 "Glory to God!" the sounding skies
    Loud with their anthems ring,—
    "Peace to the earth,—good will to men,
    From heaven's eternal King!"

5 Light on thy hills, Jerusalem!
    The Saviour now is born!
    And bright on Bethlehem's joyous plains
    Breaks the first Christmas morn.

STEPHENS. (Key A.)

1 HARK, the glad sound! the Saviour comes,—
    The Saviour, promised long;
    Let every heart prepare a throne,
    And every voice a song.

2 He comes, the pris'ner to release,
    In sinful bondage held;
    The gates of brass before him burst,
    The iron fetters yield.

3 He comes, from thickest films of vice
    To clear the mental ray
    And on the eyes oppress'd with night
    To pour celestial day.

4 He comes, the broken heart to bind,
    The wounded soul to cure,
    And, with the treasures of his grace,
    To enrich the humble poor.

5 Our glad hosannas, Prince of Peace,
    Thy welcome shall proclaim,
    And heaven's eternal arches ring
    With thy beloved name.

ZION. (Key D.)

1 ANGELS, from the realms of glory,
    Wing your flight o'er all the earth;
    Ye who sang creation's story,
    Now proclaim Messiah's birth:
        Come and worship,—
    Worship Christ, the new-born King.

2 Shepherds, in the field abiding,
    Watching o'er your flocks by night,
    God with man is now residing;
    Yonder shines the infant light:
        Come and worship,—
    Worship Christ, the new-born King.

3 Sages, leave your contemplations,—
    Brighter visions beam afar;
    Seek the great Desire of nations;
    Ye have seen his natal star:
        Come and worship,—
    Worship Christ, the new-born King.

4 Saints, before the altar bending,
    Watching long in hope and fear
    Suddenly the Lord, descending,
    In his temple shall appear:
        Come and worship,—
    Worship Christ, the new-born King.

HARK! HARK! WITH HARPS OF GOLD.

Rev. E. H. Chapin, D.D. — CHRISTMAS HYMN. — A. J. H.

1. Hark! hark! with harps of gold, What an-them do they sing? The ra-diant clouds have back-ward rolled And an-gels smite the string. "Glo - ry to God!" bright wings Spread glist'ning and a - far, And on the hal - lowed rapt - ure rings From cir - c'ling star to star.

2. "Glo - ry to God!" re - peat The glad earth and the sea; And ev' - ry wind and bil - low fleet Bears on the ju - bi - lee. Where He - brew bard hath sung Or He - brew seer hath trod, Each ho - ly spot has found a tongue: "Let glo - ry be to God."

3 Soft swells the music now
  Along that shining choir,
  And every seraph bends his brow
  And breathes above his lyre.
  What words of heavenly birth
  Thrill deep our hearts again,
  And fall like dew-drops to the earth?
  "Peace and good-will to men!"

4 Soft!—yet the soul is bound
  With rapture, like a chain:
  Earth, vocal, whispers them around,
  And heav'n repeats the strain.
  Sound, harps, and hail the morn
  With ev'ry golden string;—
  For unto us this day is born
  A Saviour and a King!

ONWARD, CHRISTIAN SOLDIERS.

S. Baring Gould. Arthur S. Sullivan.

1. Onward, Christian soldiers, Marching as to war, With the Cross of Jesus Going on before. Christ, the Royal Master, Leads against the foe: Forward into battle, See, His banners go. Onward, Christian soldiers, Marching as to war, With the cross of Jesus, Going on before.

2. Like a mighty army, Moves the Church of God: Brothers, we are treading Where the Saints have trod. We are not divided; All one body we; One in hope, in doctrine, One in charity. Onward, Christian soldiers, &c.

3 Crowns and thrones may perish,
Kingdoms rise and wane,
But the Church of Jesus
Constant will remain.
Sin and death can never
'Gainst that Church prevail:
We have Christ's own promise,
And that cannot fail.
Onward, &c.

4 Onward, then, ye faithful,
Join our happy throng,
Blend with ours your voices,
In the triumph-song:
Glory, laud, and honor,
Unto Christ the King:
This through countless ages,
Men and angels sing,
Onward, &c.

NO MORE SADNESS NOW, NOR FASTING.

CHRISTMAS SONG. ARTHUR S. SULLIVAN.

1. No more sad-ness now, nor fast-ing: Now we put our grief a-way;
God sent down the bless-ed Sav-iour, To re-joice us on this day.
Je-sus came to earth a stran-ger, Work-ing out the migh-ty plan;
And was cra-dled in a man-ger, Bring-ing life and light to man.

2. There were shep-herds once a-bid-ing In the field to watch by night,
And they saw the clouds di-vid-ing, And the sky a-bove was bright;
And a glo-ry shone a-round them On the grass as they were laid;
And a ho-ly an-gel found them, And their hearts were sore a-fraid. A-MEN.

3 "Fear ye not," he said, "for cheerful
Are the tidings that I bring;
Unto you so weak and fearful,
Christ is born, the Lord and King."
As the angel told the story
Of the Saviour's lowly birth,
Multitudes were singing "Glory
Be to God, and peace on earth!"

4 Since Thy love for our salvation,
Saviour, covered Thee with shame,
Let Thy church, in every nation,
Sing the glory of Thy Name;
Let Thy Holy Spirit make us
Full of humbleness and love,
Like Thyself, until Thou take us
To our Father's house above. AMEN.

IT CAME UPON THE MIDNIGHT CLEAR.

3 O ye beneath life's crushing load,
  Whose forms are bending low,
Who toil along the climbing way
  With painful steps and slow!
Look now, for glad and golden hours
  Come swiftly on the wing :
Oh rest beside the weary road,
  And hear the angels sing.

4 For lo, the days are hastening on,
  By prophets seen of old,
When with the ever-circling years
  Shall come the time foretold,
When the new heaven and earth shall own
  The Prince of Peace their King,
And the whole world send back the song
  Which now the angels sing.

CHRISTMAS. (Key E Flat.)

1 Awake, my soul, stretch every nerve,
  And press with vigor on;
  A heavenly race demands thy zeal,
  And an immortal crown.

2 A cloud of witnesses around
  Hold thee in full survey;
  Forget the steps already trod,
  And onward urge thy way.

3 'T is God's all animating voice,
  That calls thee from on high;
  'T is His own hand presents the prize
  To thine aspiring eye.

4 That prize, with peerless glories bright,
  Which shall new lustre boast,
  When victor's wreaths and monarch's gems
  Shall blend in common dust.

ANTIOCH. (Key E Flat.)

1 Joy to the world! the Lord is come;
  Let earth receive her King;
  Let every heart prepare Him room,
  And heaven and nature sing.

2 Joy to the world! the Saviour reigns;
  Let men their songs employ,
  While fields and floods, rocks, hills, and plains,
  Repeat the sounding joy.

3 No more let sins and sorrows grow,
  Nor thorns infest the ground;
  He comes to make His blessings flow
  As far as sin is found.

4 He rules the world with truth and grace,
  And makes the nations prove
  The glories of His righteousness,
  And wonders of His love.

BRIGHTEST AND BEST. (Key B Flat.)

1 Brightest and best of the sons of the morning,
  Dawn on our darkness, and lend us Thine aid;
  Star of the East, the horizon adorning,
  Guide where our infant Redeemer is laid.

2 Cold on His cradle the dew-drops are shining;
  Low lies His head with the beasts of the stall;
  Angels adore Him in slumber reclining,
  Maker and Monarch and Saviour of all.

3 Say, shall we yield Him, in costly devotion,
  Odors of Edom, and offerings divine,
  Gems of the mountain, and pearls of the ocean,
  Myrrh from the forest, and gold from the mine?

4 Vainly we offer each ample oblation,
  Vainly with gifts would His favor secure;
  Richer by far is the heart's adoration;
  Dearer to God are the prayers of the poor.

5 Brightest and best of the sons of the morning,
  Dawn on our darkness, and lend us Thine aid;
  Star of the East, the horizon adorning,
  Guide where our infant Redeemer is laid.

HARK! THE HERALD ANGELS.

NOW TO OUR GOD BE PRAISE.

17

Rev. Charles Follen Lee.   CHRISTMAS.   A. J. H.

3 Our foes are filled with fear,
Old Error, Sin, and Wrong;
They hear the warrant for their doom
In our glad Christmas song.
The sinner warms with hope,
The mourner dries the tear;
And every troubled heart is gay
To see our King appear.

4 Sing, then, all creatures, sing,
This long expected morn!
Praise Him from whom all goodness flows
That Christ the Lord is born!
Sing! for the weary night
At length hath worn away;
Sing! for the Saviour Prince hath come,
And this is Christmas Day.

HADDAM. (Key D.)

1 HARK ! what celestial notes,
    What melody we hear !
  Soft on the morn it floats,
    And fills the ravished ear.
The tuneful shell, | And vocal choir,
The golden lyre, | The concert swell.

2 Angelic hosts descend,
    With harmony divine ;
  See, how from heaven they bend,
    And in full chorus join !
"Fear not," say they, | Jesus, your King,
"Great joy we bring : | Is born to day."

3 "Glory to God on high !
    Ye mortals, spread the sound,
  And let your rapture fly
    To earth's remotest bound !
For peace on earth, | To man is given,
From God in heaven, | At Jesus' birth."

MERIBAH. (Key E Flat.)

1 OH, let your mingling voices rise,
    In grateful rapture, to the skies,
  And hail a Saviour's birth :
    Let songs of joy the day proclaim,
    When Jesus all-triumphant came
      To bless the sons of earth.

2 He came to bid the weary rest,
    To heal the sinner's wounded breast,
  To bind the broken heart,
    To spread the light of truth around,
    And to the world's remotest bound
      The heavenly gift impart.

3 He came our trembling souls to save
    From sin, from sorrow, and the grave,
  And chase our fears away ;
    Victorious over death and time,
    To lead us to a happier clime,
      Where reigns eternal day.

LYONS. (Key A.)

1 A VOICE from the desert comes awful and shrill ;
    The Lord is advancing ! prepare ye the way !
  The word of Jehovah He comes to fulfil,
    And o'er the dark world pour the splendor of day.

2 Bring down the proud mountain, though towering to heaven,
    And be the low valley exalted on high ;
  The rough path and crooked be made smooth and even,
    For, Zion ! your King, your Redeemer is nigh.

3 The beams of salvation His progress illume ;
    The lone, dreary wilderness sings of her Lord ;
  The rose and the myrtle there suddenly bloom,
    And the olive of peace spreads its branches abroad.

CHILDREN, SING!

2 Glad and gay
In His way,
As ye go to meet Him,
Palm leaves throw,
Garlands strow,
As a victor greet Him.
With acclaim
Sound His name,
Till, in mighty chorus,
Earth and sky
Raise the cry,
"Welcome to thine own!"

3 Prince divine!
We are thine,
Thine we are forever;
And to Thee
Pledged shall be
All our young endeavor.
Now in youth
May Thy truth
Keep our feet from straying,
And each year
Still more dear
May Thy service be.

CHRIST IS RISEN.

2 Now the iron bars are broken,
   Christ from death to life is born,—
   Glorious life, and life immortal,—
   On this holy Easter morn.
   Christ has triumphed, and we conquer
   By His mighty enterprise ;
   We with Christ to life eternal,
   By His resurrection, rise.

3 Christ is risen, we are risen :
   Shed upon us heavenly grace,
   Rain and dew, and gleams of glory,
   From the brightness of Thy face.
   Grant that we, with hearts in heaven,
   Here on earth may fruitful be,
   And by angel-hands be gathered,
   And be ever safe with Thee.

3 And as He lives, and never
　Shall taste of pain again,
　But reigns with God forever
　　To bless the sons of men,
　So we shall live, no more to die,
　When we have joined our Lord on high.
　　Sing, all ye lands, &c.

4 What token, gracious Saviour,
　May show our gratitude?
Pure hearts and meek behavior,
　And zeal for others' good.
Thus we can show our love is strong,
And raise the true disciple's song.
　　Sing all ye lands, &c.

PLEYEL'S HYMN. (Key G.)

1 CHRIST, the Lord, is risen to-day,
Our triumphant, holy day;
He endured the cross and grave,
Sinners to redeem and save.

2 Lo! he rises, mighty King!
Where, O death! is now thy sting?
Lo! he claims his native sky!
Grave! where is thy victory?

3 Christ, the Lord, is risen to-day,
Our triumphant holy day;
Loud the song of victory raise;
Shout the great Redeemer's praise.

NUREMBURG. (Key A.)

1 CHRIST the Lord is risen to-day,
Sons of men and angels say:
Raise your joys and triumphs high,
Sing, ye heavens, and earth, reply;

2 Love's redeeming work is done,
Fought the fight, the victory won:
Jesus' agony is o'er,
Darkness veils the earth no more.

3 Vain the stone, the watch, the seal,
Christ hath burst the gates of hell;
Death in vain forbids him rise;
Christ hath open'd Paradise.

4 Soar we now where Christ hath led,
Following our exalted Head;
Made like him, like him we rise;
Ours the cross, the grave, the skies.

NUREMBURG. (Key A.)

1 ANGELS, roll the rock away;
Death, yield up thy mighty prey:
See! he rises from the tomb—
Rises with immortal bloom.

2 'T is the Saviour! seraphs, raise
Your triumphant shouts of praise;
Let the earth's remotest bound
Hear the joy-inspiring sound.

3 Praise him, all ye heavenly choirs,
Praise him with your golden lyres;
Praise him in your noblest songs:
Praise him from ten thousand tongues.

PLEYEL'S HYMN. (Key G.)

1 HAIL the day that sees him rise,
Glorious, to his native skies!
Christ, awhile to mortals given,
Enters now the gates of heaven.

2 There the glorious triumph waits;
Lift your heads, eternal gates!
Christ hath vanquished death and sin;
Take the King of glory in.

3 See, the heaven our Lord receives!
Yet he loves the earth he leaves:
Though returning to his throne,
Still he calls mankind his own.

4 What, though parted from our sight,
Far above yon starry height;
Thither our affections rise,
Following him beyond the skies.

24. COME, YE FAITHFUL, RAISE THE STRAIN.

J. M. NEALE.   EASTER HYMN.   ARTHUR S. SULLIVAN.

1. Come, ye faithful, raise the strain Of triumphant gladness;
God hath brought His Israel Into joy from sadness;
Loosed from Pharaoh's bitter yoke Jacob's sons and daughters;
Led them with unmoistened foot Through the Red Sea waters. A-MEN.

2. 'Tis the spring of souls to-day; Christ hath burst His prison:
And from three days' sleep in death As a sun hath risen:
All the winter of our sins, Long and dark, is flying
From His Light, to Whom we give Laud and praise undying.

3 Now the Queen of seasons, bright
   With the Day of splendor,
   With the royal Feast of feasts,
   Comes its joys to render,
  Comes to glad Jerusalem,
   Which with true affection
  Welcomes in unwearied strains
   Jesus' Resurrection.

4 Alleluia now we cry
   To our King immortal,
  Who triumphant burst the bars
   O'er the tomb's dark portal;
  Alleluia, with the Son
   God the Father praising;
  Alleluia yet again
   To the Spirit raising. AMEN.

THE DAY OF RESURRECTION.

S. John Damascene, A.D. 780.
Trans. by J. M. Neale.

EASTER HYMN.

A. J. H.

2 Our hearts be pure from evil,
   That we may see aright
The Lord in rays eternal
   Of resurrection light;
And, listening to His accents,
   May hear, so calm and plain,
His own "All hail!" and, hearing,
   May raise the victor strain.

3 Now let the heavens be joyful!
   Let earth her song begin!
Let the round world keep triumph,
   And all that is therein!
Invisible and visible,
   Their notes let all things blend,
For Christ the Lord hath risen,
   Our Joy that hath no end.

EASTER MORNING.

A. J. H.

1. Oh, glad and bless-ed morn-ing! Oh, day of sweet sur-prise! When the an-gels watched a-dor-ing, And saw the Lord a-rise: When wo-men, bear-ing spi-ces, Came sor-rowing to the tomb, And found it full of glo-ry In-stead of death and gloom!

2. The Lord in-deed is ris-en, And death shall reign no more: He has left the grave tri-um-phant, And o-pened wide the door: Hence-forth 'tis but the cham-ber Where His wea-ry peo-ple rest... In sweet and qui-et slum-ber To rise at His be-hest.

HAIL, THOU GLORIOUS EASTER MORNING.

Anon. A. J. H.

2 Found the grave no longer bound Him,
Found death's victory was o'er;
Christ, new glory shining round Him,
Reigns in heaven forevermore. —Cho.

3 All ye nations now adore Him;
Cast your offerings at His feet;
Bring sweet flowers to lay before Him,
And glad hymns of joy repeat. —Cho.

LIFT YOUR GLAD VOICES.

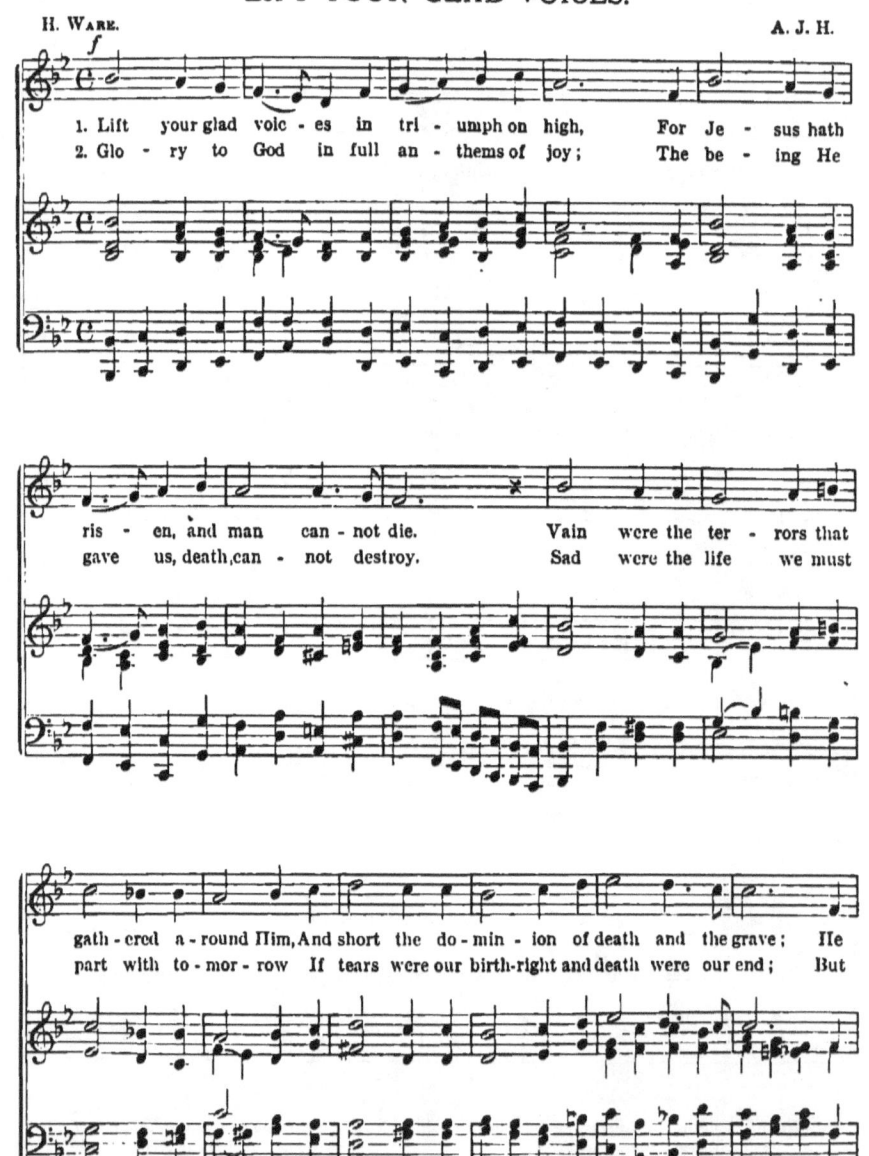

PALM SUNDAY.

REV. CHARLES FOLLEN LEE. A. J. H.

1. Who, yon humble beast bestriding, Cometh up the crowded street,
As the people with hosannas Scatter palms before His feet?
'Tis the One our fathers prayed for In the weary days of old,
Christ, the princely Son of David, Whom the prophet bards foretold.

2. Why with regal acclamations Does the holy city ring?
See we neither crown nor sceptre; Where is He they hail as King?
'Tis the meek and lowly stranger Whom the happy tribes confess;
He it is, the Lord's Anointed, King of peace and righteousness.

3 Why do jubilant ascriptions
   Burst from yonder eager throng?
Palms bespeak the warrior's trophies,
   And to conquerors belong.
He is victor, too, despoiling
   Doubt and terror, sin and woe,
And to win His greatest triumph
   Ye shall shortly see Him go.

4 Raise we, then, our loud hosannas,
   Strewing palm leaves in His way.
Blessed be the King that cometh
   To our loving hearts to-day!
Monarch, Victor, Liberator,
   Draw Thy bright unstained sword,
And in bloodless battle wield it,
   Till the world shall own Thee Lord!

ROTHWELL. (Key F.)

1 Our Lord is risen from the dead ;
   Our Jesus is gone up on high ;
   The powers of hell are captive led,—
   Dragg'd to the portals of the sky :

2 There His triumphal chariot waits,
   And angels chant the solemn lay ;—
   Lift up your heads, ye heavenly gates ;
   Ye everlasting doors, give way !

3 Loose all your bars of massy light,
   And wide unfold the' ethereal scene ;
   He claims these mansions as His right ;
   Receive the King of glory in !

4 Lo ! His triumphal chariot waits,
   And angels chant the solemn lay ;
   Lift up your heads, ye heavenly gates ;
   Ye everlasting doors, give way !

5 Who is the King of glory ? Who ?
   The Lord, of glorious power possess'd ;—
   The King of saints and angels too ;—
   God over all, forever blest !

BENEVENTO. (Key E.)

1 While with ceaseless course the sun
   Hasted through the former year,
   Many souls their race have run,
   Nevermore to meet us here :
   Fixed in an eternal state,
   They have done with all below ;
   We a little longer wait,
   But how little, none can know.

2 As the winged arrow flies
   Speedily the mark to find,
   As the lightning from the skies
   Darts and leaves no trace behind,
   Swiftly thus our fleeting days
   Bear us down life's rapid stream ;
   Upward, Lord, our spirits rise,
   All below is but a dream.

3 Thanks for mercies past receive ;
   Pardon of our sins renew ;
   Teach us, henceforth, how to live
   With eternity in view :
   Bless Thy word to young and old ;
   Fill us with a Saviour's love ;
   And when life's short tale is told,
   May we dwell with Thee above.

FEDERAL STREET. (Key A Flat.)

1 'T is by the faith of joys to come,
   We walk through deserts dark as night ;
   Till we arrive at heaven, our home,
   Faith is our guide, and faith our light.

2 The want of sight she well supplies ;
   She makes the pearly gates appear ;
   Far into distant worlds she pries,
   And brings eternal glories near.

3 Cheerful we tread the desert through
   While faith inspires a heavenly ray,
   Though lions roar, and tempests blow,
   And rocks and dangers fill the way.

NAOMI. (Key D.)

1 Father, whate'er of earthly bliss
   Thy sovereign will denies,
   Accepted at Thy throne of grace,
   Let this petition rise :

2 Give me a calm, a thankful heart,
   From every murmur free ;
   The blessings of Thy grace impart,
   And let me live to Thee.

3 Let the sweet hope that Thou art mine
   My life and death attend ;
   Thy presence through my journey shine,
   And crown my journey's end.

EASTER CHORUS.

GLEANINGS FROM THE YEAR.

Mrs. Albert Smith. A NEW YEAR'S SONG. W. C. Williams. (By per.)

1. Shine out, sun, more bright than ev-er, Sing, O birds, your sweet-est lays, While with-in God's house we gath-er On this hap-pi-est of days. Weave the freshest, sweetest flow-ers In-to garlands bright and fair, Let us make these fes-tal hours Fit for Christ himself to share; Let us make these festal hours Fit for Christ himself to share.

2. Has He not been true and ten-der To us all throughout the year; In our need, a strong de-fend-er; In temp-ta-tion, ev-er near? Have we ev-er sought Him vain-ly, Call'd Him when He turn'd a-way? That we need not miss the way? Have we ev-er sought Him vainly, Call'd Him when He turn'd a-way?

3. Oh, that there were some new tok-en, Fresh and bright, that we might bring; Some sweet lan-guage yet un-spok-en, Some new song that we might sing; Something bright saved from the hours, Act of love, or word of cheer; Ripened wheat, or fragrant flowers, Glean'd from the de-part-ed year! Ripened wheat or fragrant flow-ers, Glean'd from the departed year!

4 If for Jesus' sake we've given
  E'en a cup of water cold:
If for Him we've toiled and striven,
  He will prize it more than gold:
If we've helped an erring brother
  Back into the better way;
If we've borne with one another,
  Christ remembers it to-day!

5 Let us make such actions ours,
  For like incense they will rise
Far beyond the breath of flowers,
  Far above the sapphire skies.
Let us make the hours before us
  Beautiful with faith and cheer,
That a crown of deeds most glorious
  May adorn each closing year.

GIFTS FOR JESUS. 35

The pur - est of thought and be - hav - ior, The best of the songs that we sing.

LOUD RAISE YOUR NOTES OF JOY.

J. G. ADAMS.   FOR OUR NATIONAL ANNIVERSARY.   WM. ADRIAN SMITH.

1. Loud raise your notes of joy: Free - men, your songs em - ploy,
As well ye may;— Let your glad hearts go out In the ex -
- ult - ing shout, And with your praise de - vout, Greet this glad day.

2. Chil - dren of lisp - ing tongue, Those whose full hearts are young,
Lift up the song! Man - hood and hoar - y age, Let naught your
joy as - suage, In the high theme en - gage, Prais - es pro - long.

3. God of our fa - ther's land, Long may our tem - ples stand
Sa - cred to Thee! Let Thy bright light di - vine On all the
peo - ple shine, Make us for - ev - er Thine, From sin set free.

THE NATION'S PRAYER.

A. von Lvoff. (Russian melody.)

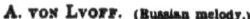

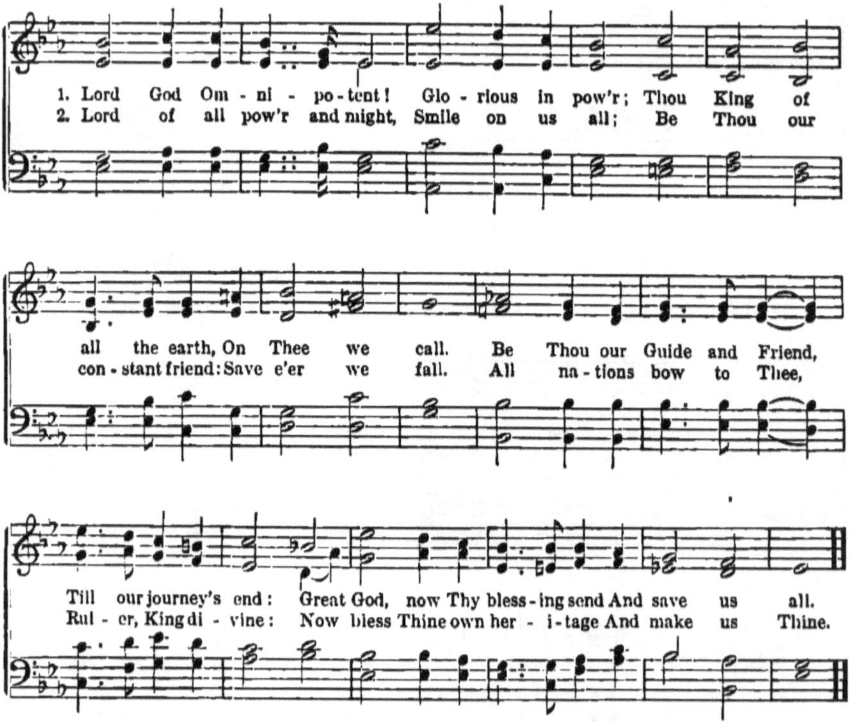
1. Lord God Om - ni - po - tent! Glo - rious in pow'r; Thou King of
2. Lord of all pow'r and might, Smile on us all; Be Thou our
all the earth, On Thee we call. Be Thou our Guide and Friend,
con - stant friend: Save e'er we fall. All na - tions bow to Thee,
Till our journey's end: Great God, now Thy bless - ing send And save us all.
Rul - er, King di - vine: Now bless Thine own her - i - tage And make us Thine.

(SECOND HYMN.)

1 Jesus, we love to meet,
  Where Thou art near;
We worship round Thy seat,
  With holy fear.
Thou tender, heavenly Friend,
To Thee our prayers ascend,
O'er our young spirits bend,
  To us draw near.

2 We dare not trifle now,
  For Thou art here:
In silent awe we bow,
  For Thou art here:
Check ev'ry wand'ring thought,
And let us all be taught
To serve Thee as we ought,
  To us be near.

3 We listen to Thy Word,
  When Thou art near;
Bless all that we have heard,
  With holy fear:
Go with us when we part,
And to each youthful heart,
Thy saving grace impart,
  Jesus, be near.

AMERICA. (Key G.)

1 My country, 't is of thee,
Sweet land of liberty,
　Of thee I sing:
Land where my fathers died,
Land of the Pilgrims' pride,
From every mountain side
　Let freedom ring!

2 My native country, thee,
Land of the noble free,
　Thy name I love:
I love thy rocks and rills,
Thy woods and templed hills;
My heart with rapture thrills
　Like that above.

3 Let music swell the breeze,
And ring from all the trees
　Sweet freedom's song;
Let mortal tongues awake,
Let all that breathe partake,
Let rocks their silence break,
　The sound prolong.

4 Our fathers' God, to Thee,
Author of liberty,
　To Thee we sing;
Long may our land be bright
With freedom's holy light,
Protect us by Thy might,
　Great God, our King!

AMERICA. (Key G.)

1 God bless our native land!
Firm may she ever stand
　Through storm and night:
When the wild tempests rave,
Ruler of wind and wave,
Do Thou our country save
　By Thy great might!

2 For her our prayer shall rise
To God, above the skies;
　On Him we wait:
Thou who art ever nigh,
Guarding with watchful eye,
To Thee aloud we cry,
　God save the State!

MAJESTY. (Key G.)

1 Ride on! ride on in majesty!
Hark! all the tribes Hosanna cry:
O Saviour meek, pursue Thy road
With palms and scattered garments strowed.

2 Ride on! ride on in majesty!
In lowly pomp, ride on to die:
O Christ, Thy triumphs now begin
O'er captive death and conquered sin.

3 Ride on! ride on in majesty!
The angel armies of the sky
Look down with sad and wondering eyes
To see the approaching sacrifice.

4 Ride on! ride on in majesty!
The last and fiercest strife is nigh:
The Father on His glorious Throne
Awaits His own anointed Son.

MISSIONARY CHANT. (Key A Flat.)

1 Lord, in Thy garden agony,
　No light seemed on Thy soul to break,
No form of seraph lingered nigh,
　Nor yet the voice of comfort spake,—

2 Till, by Thy own triumphant word,
　The victory over ill was won;
Till the sweet, mournful cry was heard,
　"Thy will, O God, not mine, be done!"

3 Lord, bring these precious moments back,
　When, fainting, against sin we strain;
Or in Thy counsels fail to track
　Aught but the present grief and pain.

In weakness, help us to contend:
　In darkness, yield to God our will:
And true hearts, faithful to the end,
　Cheer by Thy holy angels still!

JESUS, OUR COMFORTER.

Sav - iour, bless - ed Sav - iour, Keep us near Thy side,

In e - ter - nal glo - ry Ev - er to a - bide.

(SECOND HYMN.)

1 HARK, the angels, singing,
   Wake the happy morn,
  Joyful tidings bringing,
    "Christ, the Lord, is born!
  In a lowly manger—
   This shall be the sign—
  See the new-born stranger,
   Hail the Babe divine!"

2 Sisters dear, and brothers,
   Sing, O sing away!
  This above all others,
   Is the childrens' day.
  Hear its blessed story:
   "Once as young as we,
  Christ, the Prince of Glory,
   Slept on Mary's knee."

3 Where's a chorus meeter,
   For His advent here?
  Where a choral sweeter,
   To His gentle ear?
  None can come so near Him,
   Him, the undefiled,
  None so love and fear Him,
   As a Christian child.

4 In the highest regions,
   On His throne above,
  All the ransomed legions,
   Sing His matchless love:
  But of all who greet Him,
   With triumphant song,
  Little children meet Him
   In the greatest throng.

ARIEL. (Key E Flat.)

1 OH could I speak the matchless worth,
Oh could I sound the glories forth,
Which in my Saviour shine!
I'd soar, and touch the heavenly strings,
And vie with Gabriel, while he sings
In notes almost divine.

2 I'd sing the characters He bears,
And all the forms of love He wears,
Exalted on His throne:
In loftiest songs of sweetest praise,
I would, to everlasting days,
Make all His glories known.

3 Oh the delightful day will come,
When my dear Lord will bring me home,
And I shall see His face;
Then, with my Saviour, Brother, Friend,
A blest eternity I'll spend,
Triumphant in His grace.

STEPHENS. (Key A.)

1 I SING th' almighty power of God
That made the mountains rise,
That spread the flowing seas abroad,
And built the lofty skies.

2 I sing the wisdom that ordained
The sun to rule the day;
The moon shines full at His command,
And all the stars obey.

3 I sing the goodness of the Lord,
That filled the earth with food;
He formed the creatures with His word,
And then pronounced them good.

4 There's not a plant or flower below
But makes Thy glories known;
And clouds arise, and tempests blow,
By order from Thy throne.

ROTHWELL. (Key F.)

1 GREAT God, we sing that mighty hand
By which supported still we stand:
The opening year Thy mercy shows;
Let mercy crown it till it close.

2 By day, by night, at home, abroad,
Still we are guarded by our God;
By His incessant bounty fed,
By His unerring counsel led.

3 With grateful hearts the past we own;
The future, all to us unknown,
We to Thy guardian care commit,
And peaceful leave before Thy feet.

4 In scenes exalted or deprest,
Be Thou our Joy, and Thou our Rest;
Thy goodness all our hopes shall raise,
Adored through all our changing days.

LABAN. (Key C.)

1 MY soul, be on thy guard;
Ten thousand foes arise;
The hosts of sin are pressing hard
To draw Thee from the skies.

2 O watch, and fight, and pray;
The battle ne'er give o'er;
Renew it boldly every day,
And help divine implore.

3 Ne'er think the victory won,
Nor lay thine armor down:
Thy arduous work will not be done
Till thou obtain thy crown.

4 Fight on, my soul, till death
Shall bring thee to thy God;
He'll take thee at thy parting breath,
Up to His blest abode.

3 He wakes the genial spring,
  Perfumes the balmy air;
  The vales their tribute bring,
  The promise of the year.
Lift up your hearts, lift up your voice;
Rejoice, in sacred lays rejoice.

4 He leads the circling year;
  His flocks the hills adorn;
  He fills the golden ear,
  And loads the field with corn.
O happy mortals! raise your voice;
Rejoice, in sacred lays rejoice.

A SONG OF THANKSGIVING.

F. Osgood. A. J. H.

1. Approach not the altar With gloom in thy soul; Nor let thy feet falter, From terror's control! God loves not the sadness Of fear and mistrust; Oh serve Him with gladness—The Gentle, the Just.

2 His bounty is tender,
His being is love,
His smile fills with splendor
The blue arch above.
Confiding, believing,
Oh, enter always,
"His courts with thanksgiving,
His portals with praise!"

3 Nor come to the temple
With pride in thy mien,
But lowly and simple,
In courage serene,
Bring meekly before Him
The faith of a child :
Bow down and adore Him,
With heart undefiled.

HARVEST THANKSGIVING.

ARR. FROM J. A. P. SCHULTZ.

1. We plough the fields, and scat - ter The good seed on the land, But it is fed and wa - tered By God's Al-might-y hand. He sends the snow in win - ter, The warmth to swell the grain, The breez - es and the sun - shine And soft re-fresh-ing rain.
2. He on - ly is the Mak - er Of all things, near and far; He paints the way-side flow - er; He lights the even - ing star. The winds and waves o - bey Him; By Him the birds are fed; Much more to us, His chil - dren, He gives our dai - ly bread.
3. We thank Thee, then, O Fa - ther, For all things bright and good, The seed time and the har - vest, Our life, our health, our food. No gifts have we to of - fer For all Thy love im-parts, But that which Thou de - sir - est, Our hum - ble, thankful hearts!

CHORUS.

Yes, all good gifts a - round us Are sent from heav'n a - bove, Then bless and praise and thank the Lord For all His boundless love.

CORONATION. (Key G.)

1. ALL hail the power of Jesus' name!
   Let angels prostrate fall;
   Bring forth the royal diadem,
   And crown Him Lord of all.

2. Crown Him, ye martyrs of our God,
   Who from His altar call;
   Extol the Stem of Jesse's rod,
   And crown Him Lord of all.

3. Ye seed of Israel's chosen race,
   A remnant, weak and small,
   Hail Him who saves you by His grace,
   And crown Him Lord of all.

4. Sinners, whose love can ne'er forget
   The wormwood and the gall,
   Go, spread your trophies at His feet,
   And crown Him Lord of all.

5. Let every kindred, every tribe,
   On this terrestrial ball,
   To Him all majesty ascribe,
   And crown Him Lord of all.

SHIRLAND. (Key G.)

1. ARISE, and bless the Lord,
   Ye people of His choice;
   Arise, and bless the Lord your God
   With heart, and soul, and voice.

2. Though high above all praise,
   Above all blessing high,
   Who would not fear His holy Name,
   And laud, and magnify?

3. Oh for the living flame,
   From His own altar brought,
   To touch our lips, our souls inspire,
   And wing to heaven our thought.

4. God is our strength and song,
   And His salvation ours;
   Then be His love in Christ proclaim'd
   With all our ransom'd powers.

5. Arise, and bless the Lord;
   The Lord your God adore;
   Arise, and bless His glorious Name,
   Henceforth, for evermore.

SABBATH. (Key G.)

1. SAFELY through another week
   God has brought us on our way;
   Let us now a blessing seek,
   Waiting in His courts to-day;
   Day of all the week the best,
   Emblem of eternal rest!

2. While we pray for pardoning grace
   Through the dear Redeemer's Name,
   Show Thy reconciling face,
   Take away our sin and shame;
   From our worldly cares set free,
   May we rest this day in Thee.

3. Here we come Thy Name to praise;
   Let us feel Thy presence near;
   May Thy glory meet our eyes
   While we in Thy house appear:
   Here afford us, Lord, a taste
   Of our everlasting feast.

4. May Thy gospel's joyful sound
   Conquer sinners, comfort saints;
   Make the fruits of grace abound;
   Bring relief for all complaints:
   Thus let all our Sabbaths prove
   Till we rest in Thee above.

COME, YE THANKFUL PEOPLE, COME.

Dean Alford. THANKSGIVING HYMN. Sir G. J. Elvey.

3 For the Lord our God shall come,
And shall take His harvest home;
From His field shall in that day
All offences purge away;
Give His angels charge at last
Sin from out our hearts to cast;
And our love-bought souls to store
In His garner evermore.

4 Even so, Lord, quickly come,
To Thy final harvest-home;
Gather Thou Thy people in,
Free from sorrow, free from sin,
There for ever purified,
In Thy presence to abide;
Come with all Thine angels, come;
Raise the glorious harvest-home. Amen.

WE SING THE MIGHTY POWER OF GOD.

2 We sing the goodness of the Lord,
  That filled the earth with food;
  He formed the creatures with His word,
  And then pronounced them good.
  There's not a plant or flower below,
  But makes Thy glories known;
  And clouds arise, and tempests blow,
  By order from Thy throne.

THANKSGIVING DAY.

Miss F. R. Havergal. Anthony Reiff.

1. Thanks be to God! to whom earth owes Sunshine and breeze, The heath-clad hills, the vale's repose, Streamlet and seas, The snow-drop and the summer rose, The many voiced trees; The snow-drop and the summer rose, The many voiced trees.

2 Thanks for the sweetly lingering might
  In music's tone,
 For paths of knowledge whose calm light
  Is all Thine own,
 For thoughts that at the infinite
  Fold their bright wings alone.

3 Yet thanks that silence oft may flow
  In dew-like store;
 Thanks for the mysteries that show
  How small our lore;
 Thanks that we here so little know,
  And trust Thee all the more.

4 Thanks for Thine own thrice-blessed Word,
  And Sabbath rest;
 Thanks for the hope of glory stored
  In mansions blest;
 And for the Spirit's comfort poured
  Into the trembling breast.

5 Thanks, more than thanks, to Him ascend,
  Who died to win
 Our life, and every trophy rend
  From death and sin,
 Till, when the thanks of earth shall end,
  The thanks of heaven begin.

ORTONVILLE. (Key B Flat.)

1 Come, Holy Spirit, heavenly Dove,
　With all Thy quick'ning powers;
　Kindle a flame of sacred love
　In these cold hearts of ours.

2 See how we grovel here below,
　Fond of these earthly toys;
　Our souls, how heavily they go,
　To reach eternal joys.

3 In vain we tune our formal songs,—
　In vain we strive to rise:
　Hosannas languish on our tongues,
　And our devotion dies.

4 Father, and shall we ever live
　At this poor dying rate:
　Our love so faint, so cold to Thee,
　And Thine to us so great?

5 Come, Holy Spirit, heavenly Dove,
　With all Thy quick'ning powers;
　Come, shed abroad a Saviour's love,
　And that shall kindle ours.

SABBATH. (Key G.)

1 Light of life,—seraphic fire,—
　Love divine,—thyself impart;
　Every fainting soul inspire:
　Shine in every drooping heart:
　Every mournful sinner cheer;
　Scatter all our guilty gloom:
　Son of God, appear! appear!—
　To Thy human temples come.

2 Come in this accepted hour;
　Bring Thy heavenly kingdom in;
　Fill us with Thy glorious power,
　Rooting out the seeds of sin:
　Nothing more can we require,—
　We will covet nothing less;
　Be Thou all our hearts' desire,—
　All our joy and all our peace.

CORONATION. (Key G.)

1 Am I a soldier of the cross,
　A follower of the Lamb?
　And shall I fear to own His cause,
　Or blush to speak His name?

2 Must I be carried to the skies
　On flowery beds of ease,
　While others fought to win the prize,
　And sailed through bloody seas?

3 Sure I must fight if I would reign;
　Increase my courage, Lord!
　I'll bear the toil, endure the pain,
　Supported by Thy word.

4 Thy saints, in all this glorious war,
　Shall conquer though they die;
　They view the triumph from afar,
　And seize it with their eye.

5 When that illustrious day shall rise,
　And all Thine armies shine
　In robes of victory through the skies,
　The glory shall be Thine.

PARK STREET. (Key A.)

1 Wide as His vast dominion lies,
　Make the Creator's name be known;
　Loud as His thunder shout His praise,
　And sound it lofty as His throne.

2 Jehovah—'t is a glorious word!
　O, may it dwell on every tongue!
　But saints, who best have known the Lord,
　Are bound to raise the noblest song.

3 Speak of the wonders of that love
　Which Gabriel plays on every chord;
　From all below, and all above,
　Loud hallelujahs to the Lord!

DEAR LORD, REMEMBER ME.

T. Hawkis. Russian Melody.

1. Oh, Thou from whom all goodness flows, I lift my soul to Thee: In all my conflicts, sorrows, woes, Dear Lord, remember me.

2. When on my aching burdened heart My sins lie heavily, Thy pardon grant, new peace impart: Dear Lord, remember me.

3 When trials sore obstruct my way,
And ills I cannot flee,
Oh, let my strength be as my day!
Dear Lord, remember me.

4 And when before Thy throne I stand,
And lift my soul to Thee,
Then, with the saints at Thy right hand,
Dear Lord, remember me.

PRAY WITHOUT CEASING.

EDINBURG LIT. REVIEW.
ARR. FROM MOZART.

3 Or, if 't is e'er denied thee
   In solitude to pray,
 Should holy thoughts come o'er thee
   When friends are round thy way,
 E'en then the silent breathing,
   Thy spirit raised above,
 Will reach His throne of glory,
   Where dwells eternal love.

4 Oh, not a joy or blessing
   With this can we compare,—
 The grace our Father gave us
   To pour our souls in prayer:
 Whene'er thou pin'st in sadness,
   Before His footstool fall;
 Remember in thy gladness,
   His love who gave thee all.

EVENTIDE.

H. F. Lyte. W. H. Monk.

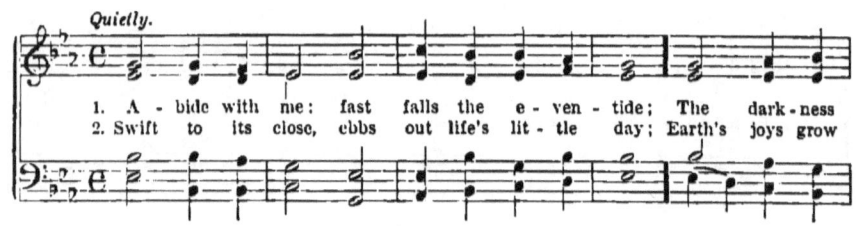
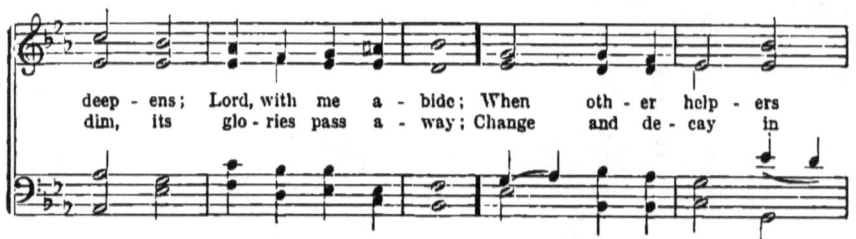

1. A-bide with me: fast falls the e-ven-tide; The dark-ness deep-ens; Lord, with me a-bide; When oth-er help-ers fail, and com-forts flee, Help of the help-less, oh, a-bide with me. A-MEN.
2. Swift to its close, ebbs out life's lit-tle day; Earth's joys grow dim, its glo-ries pass a-way; Change and de-cay in all a-round I see; O Thou who changest not, a-bide with me.

3 I need Thy presence every passing hour;
What but Thy grace can foil the tempter's power?
Who like Thyself my guide and stay can be?
Through cloud and sunshine, Lord, abide with me.

4 I fear no foe, with Thee at hand to bless;
Ills have no weight, and tears no bitterness;
Where is death's sting? where, grave, thy victory?
I triumph still, if thou abide with me.

5 Hold Thou Thy Cross before my closing eyes;
Shine through the gloom, and point me to the skies;
Heaven's morning breaks, and earth's vain shadows flee;
In life, in death, O Lord, abide with me.

EVENING PRAYER.

C. WINKWORTH.   FLEMMING.

1. Now, God, be with us, for the night is closing;
The light and darkness are of His disposing;
And 'neath His shadow here to rest we yield us,
For He will shield us.

2 Let evil thoughts and spirits flee before us;
Till morning cometh, watch, O Father, o'er us;
In soul and body Thou from harm defend us;
Thine angels send us.

3 We have no refuge, none on earth to aid us,
But Thee, O Father, who Thine own hast made us:
Keep us in life; forgive our sins; deliver
Us evermore. Amen.

COME, LET US PRAY.

2 Come, let us pray: the burning brow,
   The heart oppressed with care,
   And all the woes that throng us now,
   Will be relieved by prayer;
   Our God will chase our griefs away;
   Oh, glorious thought!— come, let us pray.

3 Come, let us pray: the mercy-seat
   Invites the fervent prayer,
   Our Heavenly Father waits to greet
   The contrite spirit there:
   Oh, loiter not, nor longer stay
   From Him who loves us: let us pray.

AMSTERDAM. (Key G.)

1 Rise, my soul, and stretch thy wings,
  Thy better portion trace;
Rise from transitory things
  Towards heaven, thy native place:
Sun and moon and stars decay;
  Time shall soon this earth remove;
Rise, my soul, and haste away
  To seats prepared above.

2 Rivers to the ocean run,
  Nor stay in all their course;
Fire, ascending, seeks the sun;
  Both speed them to their source:
So a soul that's born of God,
  Pants to view His glorious face,
Upward tends to His abode,
  To rest in His embrace.

3 Cease, ye pilgrims, cease to mourn;
  Press onward to the prize;
Soon our Saviour will return
  Triumphant in the skies:
Yet a season, and we know
  Happy entrance will be given,
All our sorrows left below,
  And earth exchanged for heaven.

AMSTERDAM. (Key G.)

1 Open, Lord, my inward ear,
  And bid my heart rejoice:
Bid my quiet spirit hear
  Thy comfortable voice;
Never in the whirlwind found,
  Or where earthquakes rock the place,
Still and silent is the sound,
  The whisper of Thy grace.

2 From the world of sin, and noise,
  And hurry, I withdraw;
For the small and inward voice
  I wait with humble awe:
Silent am I now and still;
  Dare not in Thy presence move;
To my waiting soul reveal
  The secret of Thy love.

3 Thou didst undertake for me;
  For me to death wast sold;
Wisdom in a mystery
  Of bleeding love unfold;
Teach the lesson of Thy cross:
  Let me die, with Thee to reign!
All things let me count but loss
  So I may Thee regain!

LISBON. (Key A.)

1 Come, kingdom of our God,
  Sweet reign of light and love!
Shed peace, and hope, and joy abroad,
  And wisdom from above.

2 Over our spirits first
  Extend Thy healing reign;
There raise and quench the sacred thirst
  That never pains again.

3 Come, kingdom of our God,
  And make the broad earth Thine;
Stretch o'er her lands and isles the rod
  That flowers with grace divine.

4 Soon may all tribes be blest
  With fruit from life's glad tree;
And in its shade like brothers rest,
  Sons of one family.

PRAYER OF THE SABBATH SCHOOL CHILDREN.

Mrs. C. M. Sawyer.   A. J. H.

1. Father, Thou who art in heaven, O'er us brood in love to-day; Let Thy truth our spir-it leav-en, While our young lips sing and pray: Gathered in Thy ho-ly tem-ple, Low our youth-ful hearts we bow! By Thy lov-ing, pure ex-am-ple, Sa-viour, King, in-spire us now.

2. Make our love deep, true, out-reach-ing, Clasping all where'er they be! Make our lives like an-gels preaching, Strong to lead the lost to Thee; Oh the thousand streets and al-leys; Oh the sea-isles far a-way! Oh the countless hills and val-leys, Where they know not Thee to-day!

3 Shall they walk thus, blindly groping
Down the paths of sin and death?
Shall they like dumb brutes, unhoping,
'Mid the darkness yield their breath?
What to them, tho' Thou in Zion
On the cross for love's sake died,
If they know not that, in dying,
Thou for them wert crucified!

4 Nay! we know tho' long averted,
Father, though Thine eyes may be,
Never yet was one deserted,
Ne'er will one be lost by Thee!
Peace our hearts! Oh, triumph, rather,
Of this last great solace sure;
In Thine own good time, O Father,
Ev'ry ill will find a cure.

THE LORD'S PRAYER. No. 1.

SARAH J. HALE. A. J. H.

ST. THOMAS. (Key G.)

1 Stand up and bless the Lord,
   Ye people of His choice;
   Stand up, and bless the Lord your God,
   With heart, and soul, and voice.

2 Though high above all praise,
   Above all blessing high,
   Who would not fear His holy name,
   And laud and magnify?

3 Oh, for the living flame
   From His own altar brought,
   To touch our lips, our minds inspire,
   And wing to heaven our thought!

4 There, with benign regard,
   Our hymns He deigns to hear;
   Though unrevealed to mortal sense,
   The spirit feels Him near.

STEPHENS. (Key A.)

1 Blest day of God! most calm, most bright,
   The first and best of days;
   The laborer's rest, the saint's delight,
   The day of prayer and praise.

2 My Saviour's face made thee to shine;
   His rising thee did raise;
   And made thee heavenly and divine
   Beyond all other days.

3 The first fruits oft a blessing prove
   To all the sheaves behind;
   And they who do the Sabbath love,
   A happy week will find.

4 This day I must to God appear;
   For, Lord, the day is Thine;
   Help me to spend it in Thy fear,
   And thus to make it mine.

PLEYEL'S HYMN. (Key G.)

1 Children of the heavenly King,
   As we journey let us sing;
   Sing our Saviour's worthy praise,
   Glorious in His works and ways.

2 We are trav'ling home to God,
   In the way our fathers trod;
   They are happy now, and we
   Soon their happiness shall see.

3 Fear not, brethren, joyful stand
   On the borders of our land;
   Jesus Christ, our Father's Son,
   Bids us undismay'd go on.

4 Lord! obediently we'll go,
   Gladly leaving all below:
   Only Thou our leader be,
   And we still will follow Thee.

DUKE STREET. (Key F.)

1 Jesus shall reign where'er the sun
   Does his successive journeys run;
   His kingdom stretch from shore to shore,
   Till moons shall wax and wane no more.

2 For Him shall endless prayer be made,
   And praises throng to crown His head;
   His name like sweet perfume shall rise
   With every morning sacrifice.

3 People and realms of every tongue
   Dwell on His love with sweetest song;
   And infant voices shall proclaim
   Their early blessings on His Name.

4 Let every creature rise and bring
   Peculiar honors to our king;
   Angels descend with songs again,
   And earth repeat the loud Amen!

O PARADISE! No. 1.

F. W. Faber. Joseph Barnby.

3 O Paradise! O Paradise!
  We want to sin no more;
  We want to be as pure on earth
  As on thy spotless shore.—Cho.

4 Lord Jesus, Prince of Paradise!
  Oh, keep us in Thy love,
  And guide us to that happy land
  Of perfect rest above.—Cho.

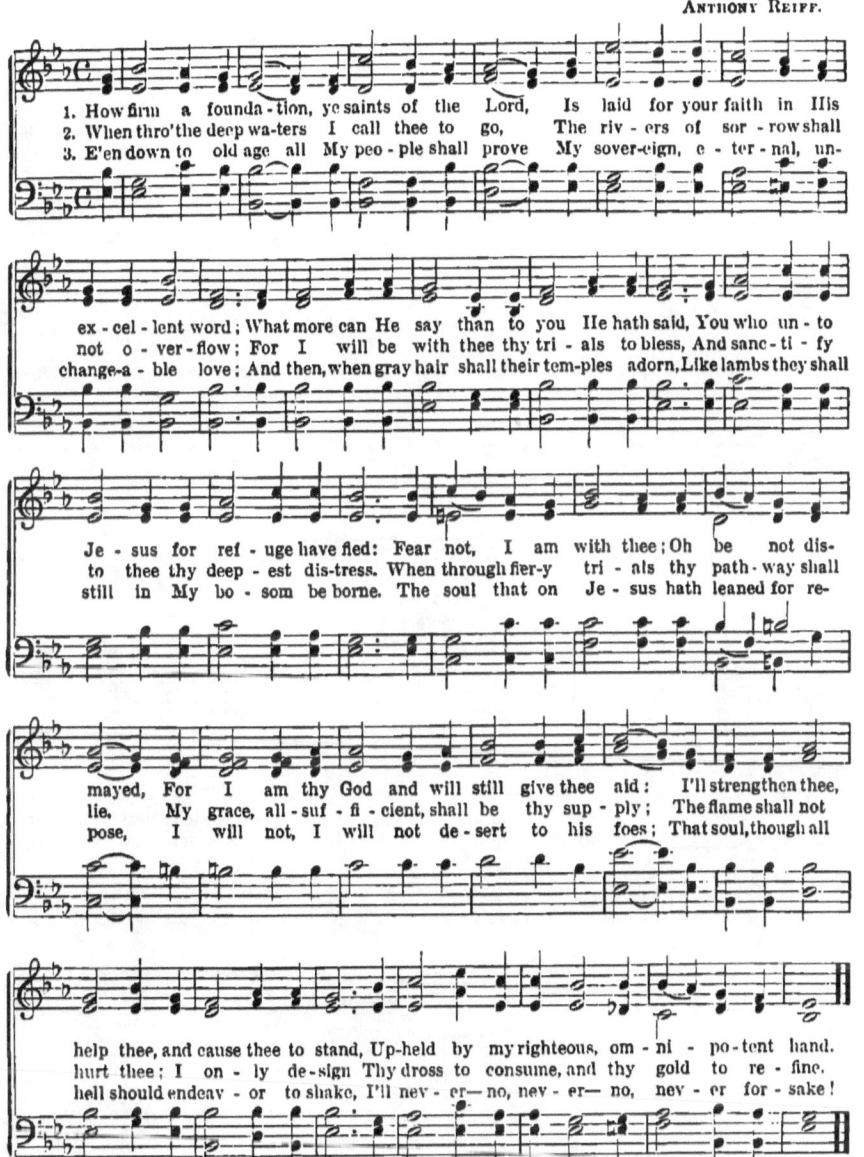

DUNDEE. (Key F.)

1 God moves in a mysterious way,
  His wonders to perform;
  He plants His footsteps in the sea,
  And rides upon the storm.

2 Deep in unfathomable mines
  Of never failing skill,
  He treasures up His bright designs,
  And works His sov'reign will.

3 Ye fearful saints, fresh courage take:
  The clouds ye so much dread
  Are big with mercy, and shall break
  In blessings on your head.

4 Judge not the Lord by feeble sense,
  But trust Him for His grace;
  Behind a frowning providence
  He hides a smiling face.

5 His purposes will ripen fast,
  Unfolding every hour:
  The bud may have a bitter taste,
  But sweet will be the flower.

6 Blind unbelief is sure to err,
  And scan His work in vain:
  God is His own interpreter,
  And He will make it plain.

SICILY. (Key F.)

1 Lord, dismiss us with Thy blessing,
  Fill our hearts with joy and peace;
  Let us each, Thy love possessing,
  Triumph in redeeming grace;
    O refresh us,
  Travelling through this wilderness.

2 Thanks we give, and adoration,
  For Thy gospel's joyful sound;
  May the fruit of Thy salvation
  In our hearts and lives abound:
    May Thy presence
  With us evermore be found.

SHIRLAND. (Key G.)

1 Blest be the tie that binds
  Our hearts in Christian love;
  The fellowship of kindred minds
  Is like to that above.

2 Before our Father's throne
  We pour our ardent prayers;
  Our fears, our hopes, our aims are one,—
  Our comforts and our cares.

3 We share our mutual woes;
  Our mutual burdens bear;
  And often for each other flows
  The sympathizing tear.

4 When we asunder part,
  It gives us inward pain;
  But we shall still be joined in heart,
  And hope to meet again.

5 This glorious hope revives
  Our courage by the way;
  While each in expectation lives
  And longs to see the day.

6 From sorrow, toil, and pain,
  And sin we shall be free;
  And perfect love and friendship reign
  Through all eternity.

OLD HUNDRED. (Key G.)

1 From all that dwell below the skies,
  Let the Creator's praise arise;
  Let the Redeemer's name be sung
  Through every land, by every tongue.

2 Eternal are Thy mercies, Lord;
  Eternal truth attends Thy word;
  Thy praise shall sound from shore to shore
  Till suns shall rise and set no more.

4 Rest comes at length, though life be long and dreary,
   The day must dawn, and darksome night be past;
   All journeys end in welcome to the weary,
   And heaven, the heart's true home, will come at last.—Cho.

5 Angels, sing on! your faithful watches keeping;
   Sing us sweet fragments of the songs above;
   Till morning's joy shall end the night of weeping,
   And life's long shadows break in cloudless love.—Cho.

HAIL TO THE LORD'S ANOINTED.

J. Montgomery.   A. J. H.

1. Hail to the Lord's A-noint - ed, Great Da-vid's great - er Son! Hail, in the time ap-point - ed, His reign on earth be - gun; He comes to break op - pres - sion, To set the cap - tive free; To take a - way trans - gres - sion And rule in e - qui - ty.

2. He comes with suc - cor speed - y To those that suf - fer wrong, To help the poor and need - y, And bid the weak be strong: To give them songs for sigh - ing, Their dark- ness turn to light, Whose souls, condemn'd and dy - ing Were pre - cious in His sight.

3 He shall descend like showers
  Upon the fruitful earth;
And love and joy, like flowers,
  Spring in His path to birth:
Before Him, on the mountains,
  Shall peace, the herald, go;
And righteousness, in fountains,
  From hill to valley flow.

4 To Him shall prayer unceasing
  And daily vows ascend;
His kingdom still increasing,
  A kingdom without end:
The tide of time shall never
  His covenant remove;
His name shall stand forever;
  That name to us is Love.

LISCHER. (Key G.)

1 WELCOME, delightful morn,
  Thou day of sacred rest;
  I hail thy kind return.
  Lord, make these moments blest!
  From the low train of mortal toys
  I soar to reach immortal joys.

2 Now may the King descend
  And fill His throne of grace:
  Thy sceptre, Lord, extend,
  While saints address Thy face:
  Let sinners feel Thy quickening word,
  And learn to know and fear the Lord.

3 Descend, celestial Dove,
  With all Thy quickening powers;
  Disclose a Saviour's love,
  And bless the sacred hours:
  Then shall my soul new life obtain,
  Nor Sabbaths be indulged in vain.

ZION. (Key D.)

1 GUIDE me, O thou great Jehovah,
  Pilgrim through this mortal land:
  I am weak, but Thou art mighty;
  Hold me with Thy powerful hand:
  Bread of heaven,
  Feed me till I want no more.

2 Open now the crystal fountain,
  Whence the healing streams do flow;
  Let the fiery, cloudy pillar
  Lead me all my journey through:
  Strong Deliverer,
  Be Thou still my Strength and Shield.

3 When I tread the verge of Jordan,
  Bid my anxious fears subside;
  Bear me through the swelling current;
  Land me safe on Canaan's side:
  Songs of praises
  I will ever give to Thee.

HENDON. (Key G.)

1 GRACIOUS Spirit, Love divine!
  Let Thy light within me shine;
  All my guilty fears remove;
  Fill me with Thy heavenly love.

2 Speak Thy pard'ning grace to me;
  Set the burden'd sinner free;
  Lead me to the Lamb of God;
  Wash me in His precious blood.

3 Life and peace to me impart;
  Seal salvation on my heart;
  Breathe Thyself into my breast,—
  Earnest of immortal rest.

4 Let me never from Thee stray;
  Keep me in the narrow way;
  Fill my soul with joy divine;
  Keep me, Lord, forever Thine.

DEDHAM. (Key A.)

1 HOLY and reverend is the name
  Of our eternal King;
  Thrice holy Lord, the angels cry;
  Thrice holy, let us sing.

2 The deepest reverence of the mind
  Pay, O my soul, to God;
  Lift with thy hands a holy heart
  To His sublime abode.

3 With sacred awe pronounce His name,
  Whom words nor thoughts can reach;
  A broken heart shall please Him more
  Than the best forms of speech.

4 Thou holy God! preserve my soul
  From all pollution free;
  The pure in heart are Thy delight,
  And they Thy face shall see.

ABOVE THE CLEAR BLUE SKY.

3 O Blessed Lord, Thy truth
To us, Thy babes, impart ;
And teach us in our youth
To know Thee as Thou art.
Alleluia !
Then shall we sing
To God our King,
Alleluia !

4 Oh ! may Thy holy word
Spread all the world around ;
And all with one accord
Uplift the joyful sound.
Alleluia !
All then shall sing
To God their King,
Alleluia ! Amen.

O PARADISE! No. 2.

F. G. Ilsley.

3 O Paradise, O Paradise,
  'Tis weary waiting here;
I long to be where Jesus is,
  To feel, to see Him near;
Where loyal hearts and true, &c.

4 O Paradise, O Paradise,
  I want to sin no more;
I want to be as pure on earth
  As on thy spotless shore;
Where loyal hearts and true, &c.

COURAGE.

3 One the strain the lips of thousands
 Lift as from the heart of one;
One the conflict, one the peril,
 One the march in God begun;
One the gladness of rejoicing
 On the far eternal shore.
Where the one Almighty Father
 Reigns in love for evermore.

4 Onward, therefore, pilgrim brothers,
 Onward with the Cross our aid!
Bear its shame, and fight its battle,
 Till we rest beneath its shade!
Soon shall come the great awaking,
 Soon the rending of the tomb;
Then, the scattering of all shadows,
 And the end of toil and gloom!

HOLY BIBLE, BOOK DIVINE.

2 Mine, to chide me when I rove;
  Mine, to show a Saviour's love;
  Mine art thou to guide my feet;
  Mine, to judge, condemn, acquit;

3 Mine, to comfort in distress,
  If the Holy Spirit bless;
  Mine, to show by living faith
  Man can triumph over death:

WHAT A FRIEND WE HAVE IN JESUS. (Key F.)

1 What a Friend we have in Jesus
  All our sins and griefs to bear!
  What a privilege to carry
  Everything to God in prayer!
  Oh, what peace we often forfeit,
  Oh, what needless pain we bear—
  All because we do not carry
  Everything to God in prayer!

2 Have we trials and temptations?
  Is there trouble anywhere?
  We should never be discouraged;
  Take it to the Lord in prayer.
  Can we find a Friend so faithful,
  Who will all our sorrows share?
  Jesus knows our every weakness;
  Take it to the Lord in prayer.

3 Are we weak and heavy laden,
  Cumbered with a load of care?
  Precious Saviour, still our Refuge!
  Take it to the Lord in prayer.
  Do thy friends despise, forsake thee?
  Take it to the Lord in prayer;
  In His arms He'll take and shield thee;
  Thou wilt find a solace there.

ITALIAN HYMN. (Key G.)

1 Come, Thou almighty King,
   Help us Thy name to sing,
     Help us to praise:
   Father all glorious,
   O'er all victorious,
   Come, and reign over us,
     Ancient of days.

2 Come, Thou incarnate Word,
   Gird on Thy mighty sword,
     Our prayer attend;
   Come, and Thy people bless,
   And give Thy word success:
   Spirit of holiness,
     On us descend.

3 Come, holy Comforter,
   Thy sacred witness bear
     In this glad hour:
   Thou who almighty art,
   Now rule in every heart,
   And ne'er from us depart,
     Spirit of power.

BETHANY. (Key G.)

1 No, not despairingly
    Come I to Thee;
   No, not distrustingly
    Bend I the knee;
   Sin hath gone over me;
   Yet is this still my plea,
    Jesus hath died.

2 Lord, I confess to Thee
    Sadly my sin;
   All I am, tell I Thee;
    All I have been;
   Purge Thou my sin away;
   Wash Thou my soul this day;
    Lord, make me clean.

3 Faithful and just art Thou,
    Forgiving all;
   Loving and kind art Thou
    When poor ones call;
   Lord, let the cleansing blood,
   Blood of the Lamb of God,
    Pass o'er my soul!

UXBRIDGE. (Key E Flat.)

1 The heavens declare Thy glory, Lord,
   In every star Thy wisdom shines;
  But when our eyes behold Thy word,
   We read Thy name in fairer lines.

2 The rolling sun, the changing light,
   And nights and days Thy power confess;
  But the blest volume Thou hast writ
   Reveals Thy justice and Thy grace.

3 Sun, moon, and stars convey Thy praise
   Round the whole earth, and never stand;
  So when Thy truth began its race,
   It touched and glanced on every land.

4 Nor will Thy spreading gospel rest,
   Till through the world Thy truth has run;
  Till Christ has all the nations blest,
   That see the light, or feel the sun.

5 Great Sun of righteousness, arise;
   Bless the dark world with heavenly light;
  Thy gospel makes the simple wise;
   Thy laws are pure, Thy judgments right.

6 Thy noblest wonders here we view,
   In souls renewed and sins forgiven;
  Lord, cleanse my sins, my soul renew,
   And make Thy word my guide to heaven.

FORWARD! BE OUR WATCHWORD.

4 Glories upon glories
  Hath our God prepared,
  By the souls that love Him
  One day to be shared ;
  Eye hath not beheld them,
  Ear hath never heard,
  Nor of these hath uttered
    Thought or speech a word ;
    Forward marching eastward
    Where the heaven is bright,
    Till the veil be lifted,
    Till our faith be sight !

5 Far o'er yon horizon
  Rise the city towers,
  Where our God abideth ;
  That fair home is ours :
  Flash the streets with jasper,
  Shine the gates with gold,
  Flows the gladdening river
  Shedding joys untold :
    Thither, onward thither,
    In the Spirit's might :
    Pilgrims to your country,
    Forward into Light !

6 Into God's high temple
  Onward as we press,
  Beauty spreads around us,
  Born of holiness ;
  Arch, and vault, and carving,
  Lights of varied tone ;
  Softened words and holy,
  Prayer and praise alone ;
  Every thought upraising
    To our City bright,
    Where the tribes assemble
    Round the throne of Light.

7 Nought that city needeth
  Of these aisles of stone :
  Where the Godhead dwelleth,
  Temple there is none.
  All the saints that ever
  In these courts have stood,
  Are but babes, and feeding
  On the children's food,
  On through sign and token,
    Stars amidst the night :
    Forward through the darkness,
    Forward into Light !

SUPPLIANT, LO! THY CHILDREN BEND.

GREY. A. J. H.

1. Sup-pliant, lo! Thy chil-dren bend, Fa-ther, for Thy bless-ing now;
Thou canst teach us, guide, de-fend; We are weak, Al-might-y Thou.

2 With the peace Thy word imparts,
  Be the taught and teacher blest ;
  In our lives and on our hearts,
  Father, be Thy laws impressed.

3 Pour into each longing mind
  Light and knowledge from above ;
  Charity for all mankind,
  Trusting faith, enduring love.

FORWARD! BE OUR WATCHWORD. No. 2.

DEAN ALFORD. *Boldly.* HENRY SMART.

1. Forward! be our watch-word, Steps and voic-es joined; Seek the things be-fore us,
Not a look be-hind. Burns the fier-y pil-lar At our ar-my's head;
Who shall dream of shrink-ing, By our Cap-tain led? Forward thro' the des-ert,
Thro' the toil and fight: Jordan flows be-fore us, Si-on beams with light. A-MEN.

2. Forward, when in child-hood Buds the in-fant mind; All thro' youth and man-hood,
Not a thought be-hind: Speed thro' realms of na-ture; Climb the steps of grace;
Faint not, till in glo-ry Gleams our Father's face. Forward, all the life-time
Climb from height to height, Till the head be hoar-y, Till the eve be light.

3 Forward, flock of Jesus,
Salt of all the earth,
Till each yearning purpose
Spring to glorious birth;
Sick, they ask for healing,
Blind, they grope for day;
Pour upon the nations
Wisdom's loving ray.
Forward, out of error,
Leave behind the night;
Forward through the darkness,
Forward into light.

4 Glories upon glories,
Hath our God prepared,
By the souls that love Him
One day to be shared;
Eye hath not beheld them,
Ear hath never heard;
Nor of these hath uttered
Thought or speech or word.
Forward marching eastward
Where the heaven is bright,
Till the veil be lifted,
Till our faith be sight!

SILVER STREET. (Key C.)

1 Come, sound His praise abroad,
   And hymns of glory sing:
   Jehovah is the sov'reign God,
   The universal King.

2 He form'd the deeps unknown;
   He gave the seas their bound;
   The wat'ry worlds are all His own,
   And all the solid ground.

3 Come, worship at His throne,
   Come, bow before the Lord;
   We are His works, and not our own,
   He form'd us by His word.

4 To-day attend His voice,
   Nor dare provoke His rod;
   Come, like the people of His choice,
   And own your gracious God.

SPOHR. (Key E.)

1 Thy presence, gracious God, afford;
   Prepare us to receive Thy word:
   Now let Thy voice engage our ear,
   And faith be mix'd with what we hear.

2 Distracting thoughts and cares remove,
   And fix our hearts and hopes above;
   With food divine may we be fed,
   And satisfied with living bread.

3 To us the sacred word apply,
   With sov'reign power and energy;
   And may we, in Thy faith and fear,
   Reduce to practice what we hear.

4 Father, in us Thy Son reveal:
   Teach us to know and do Thy will:
   Thy saving power and love display,
   And guide us to the realms of day.

LYONS. (Key A.)

1 O, worship the King, all glorious above,
   And gratefully sing His wonderful love;
   Our Shield and Defender, the Ancient of Days,
   Pavilion'd in splendor, and girded with praise.

2 Thy bountiful care what tongue can recite?
   It breathes in the air, it shines in the light,
   It streams from the hills, it descends to the plain,
   And sweetly distils in the dew and the rain.

3 Frail children of dust, and feeble as frail,
   In Thee do we trust, nor find Thee to fail;
   Thy mercies how tender! how firm to the end!
   Our Maker, Defender, Redeemer, and Friend.

4 O Father almighty, how faithful Thy love!
   While angels delight to hymn Thee above,
   The humbler creation, though feeble their lays
   With true adoration shall lisp to Thy praise.

SEASONS. (Key G.)

1 How sweetly flow'd the gospel's sound
   From lips of gentleness and grace,
   While list'ning thousands gather'd round,
   And joy and reverence fill'd the place.

2 From heaven He came, of heaven He spoke.
   To heaven He lead His foll'wers' way;
   Dark clouds of gloomy night he broke,
   Unveiling an immortal day.

3 Come, wand'rers, to my Father's home;
   Come, all ye weary ones, and rest.
   Yes, sacred Teacher! we will come,
   Obey, and be forever blest.

4 Decay, then, tenements of dust!
   Pillars of earthly pride, decay!
   A nobler mansion waits the just,
   And Jesus has prepared the way.

WE MARCH TO VICTORY.

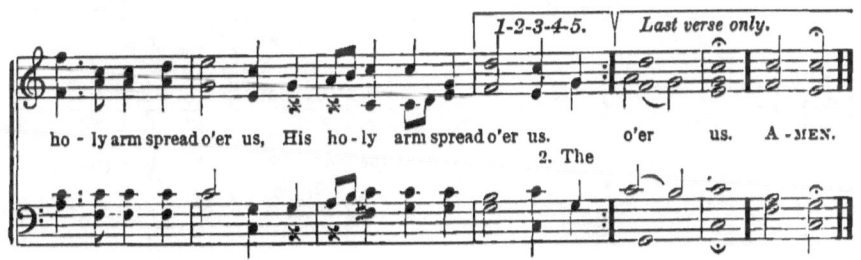

3 Our sword is the Spirit of God on High,
  Our helmet His Salvation :
  Our banner the Cross of Calvary.
  Our watchword—The Incarnation.—Cho.

4 He marches in front of His banner unfurled,
  Which He raised that His own might find Him;
  And the Holy Church throughout the world
  Fall into rank behind Him.—Cho.

5 And the choir of angels with songs awaits
  Our march to the golden Sion ;
  For our Captain has broken the brazen gates,
  And burst the bars of iron.—Cho.

6 Then onward we march, our arms to prove,
  With the banner of Christ before us,
  With His eye of love looking down from above,
  And His holy arm spread o'er us.—Cho.

WE MARCH TO VICTORY. No. 2.

F. G. Ilsley.

1. We march, we march to vic-to-ry With the cross of the Lord be-fore us,
With His lov-ing eye look-ing down from the sky, And His ho-ly arm spread o'er us.

CHORUS *after each verse.*
We march, we march to vic-to-ry, With the cross of the Lord be-fore us,
We march, we march to vic-to-ry With the cross of the Lord be-fore us.

2 We come in the might of the Lord of light,
  With joyful songs to meet Him,
  And we put to flight the armies of night
  That the sons of day may greet Him.—Cho.

3 The bands of the Alien flee away,
  When our chant goes up like thunder;
  And the van of the Lord in serried array
  Cleaves Satan's ranks asunder.—Cho.

4 Our sword is the Spirit of God on high,
  Our helmet is His salvation,
  Our banner the Cross of Calvary,
  Our watchword—The Incarnation.—Cho.

5 And the choir of angels with song awaits
  Our march to the golden Sion;
  For our Captain has broken the brazen gates,
  And burst the bars of iron.—Cho.

6 Then onward we march, our arms to prove,
  With the banner of Christ before us,
  With His eye of love looking down from above,
  And His holy arm spread o'er us.—Cho.

7 We march, we march to victory!
  With the cross of the Lord before us,
  With His loving eye looking down from the sky,
  And His holy arm spread o'er us. Amen.

THE CHRISTIAN SOLDIER.

3 Stand up! stand up for Jesus!
   Stand in His strength alone;
   The arm of flesh will fail you;
   Ye dare not trust your own;
   Put on the gospel armor,
   And, watching unto prayer,
   Where duty calls, or danger,
   Be never wanting there.

4 Stand up! stand up for Jesus!
   The strife will not be long;
   This day the noise of battle,
   The next the victor's song.
   To him that overcometh,
   A crown of life shall be;
   He with the King of Glory
   Shall reign eternally!

CREATION'S SOVEREIGN LORD!

J. G. Adams.
A. J. H.

1. Cre-a-tion's sov-'reign Lord! Be Thy glad name a-dored Though earth and sky! Hear, as in youthful days... To Thee we humbly raise,... Songs of our grateful praise,...... Holy and high.
2. Thanks for Thy light so free, Caus-ing our eyes to see Thy truth and grace; Love that dispels our fear,... Mer-cy, to sin-ners dear,... Life, dy-ing souls to cheer,...... For all our race.

3 Thanks, that on hearts like ours
Thy loving kindness showers
Knowledge divine :
O let its influence be
Fruitful in works for Thee,
Causing in purity
Our lives to shine.

4 Bless this our childhood band,
And let us ever stand
Truthful and strong ;
Christians in deed and love
Such as thou wilt approve,
Till we in worlds above
Thy praise prolong !

STERLING. (Key A.)

1 Oh, come, loud anthems let us sing,
    Loud thanks to our almighty King;
    For we our voices high should raise,
    When our Salvation's Rock we praise.

2 Into His presence let us haste,
    To thank Him for His favors past:
    To Him address, in joyful songs,
    The praise that to His name belongs.

3 Oh, let us to His courts repair,
    And bow with adoration there;
    With joy and fear devoutly all
    Before the Lord, our Maker, fall!

MAGNUS. (Key A.)

1 WALK in the light; so shalt thou know
    That fellowship of love,
    His Spirit only can bestow
    Who reigns in light above.

2 Walk in the light! and thou shalt find
    Thy heart made truly His
    Who dwells in cloudless light enshrined,
    In whom no darkness is.

3 Walk in the light! and thou shalt own
    Thy darkness pass'd away,
    Because that Light hath on thee shone
    In which is perfect day.

4 Walk in the light! and e'en the tomb
    No fearful shade shall wear;
    Glory shall chase away its gloom,
    For Christ hath conquer'd there.

5 Walk in the light! thy path shall be
    Peaceful, serene, and bright:
    For God, by grace, shall dwell in thee,
    And God himself is light.

GERMANY. (Key B Flat.)

1 JESUS, the gift divine I know,
    The gift divine I ask of Thee:
    The living water now bestow,
    Thy Spirit and thyself, on me.

2 For Thou of life the fountain art,
    None else can give or take away;
    Oh, may I feel it in my heart,
    And with me may it ever stay.

3 Thus may I drink, and thirst no more
    For drops of finite happiness;
    Spring up, O well, in heavenly power,
    In streams of pure perennial peace.

DUKE ST. (Key F.)

1 GREAT God! beneath whose piercing eye
    The earth's extended kingdom's lie;
    Whose fav'ring smile upholds them all,
    Whose anger smites them, and they fall;

2 We bow before Thy heavenly throne;
    Thy power we see, Thy greatness own;
    Yet, cherish'd by Thy milder voice,
    Our bosoms tremble and rejoice.

3 Thy kindness to our fathers shown
    Their children's children long shall own;
    To Thee, with grateful hearts, shall raise
    The tribute of exulting praise.

4 Led on by Thine unerring aid,
    Secure the paths of life we tread;
    And, freely as the vital air,
    Thy first and noblest bounties share.

5 Great God, our Guardian, Guide, and Friend!
    Oh, still Thy sheltering arm extend;
    Preserved by Thee for ages past,
    For ages let Thy kindness last!

4 I fear no foe, with Thee at hand to bless:
Ills have no weight, and tears no bitterness.
Where is death's sting? where, grave, thy victory?
I triumph still, if Thou abide with me.

5 Hold Thou Thy cross before my closing eyes;
Shine through the gloom and point me to the skies;
Heaven's morning breaks, and earth's vain shadows flee;
In life, in death, O Lord, abide with me.

FEDERAL STREET. (Key A Flat.)

1 Come, gracious Spirit, heavenly Dove,
With light and comfort from above;
Be Thou my Guardian, Thou my Guide;
O'er every thought and step preside.

2 The light of truth to me display,
And make me know and choose Thy way;
Plant holy fear within my heart,
That I from Thee may ne'er depart.

3 Conduct me safe, conduct me far
From every sin and hurtful snare;
Lead me to God, my final rest,
In His enjoyment to be blest.

4 Lead me to Christ, the living way,
Nor let me from His pastures stray;
Lead me to heaven, the seat of bliss,
Where pleasure in perfection is.

PLEYEL'S HYMN. (Key G.)

1 Holy Spirit, truth divine!
Dawn upon this soul of mine;
Son of God, and inward light!
Wake my spirit, clear my sight!

2 Holy Spirit, power divine!
Fill and nerve this will of mine;
By Thee may I strongly live,
Bravely bear and nobly strive.

3 Holy Spirit, love divine!
Glow within this heart of mine;
Kindle every high desire;
Perish self in Thy pure fire!

4 Holy Spirit, peace divine!
Still this restless heart of mine;
Speak to calm this tossing sea,
Stayed in Thy tranquillity.

PORTUGUESE HYMN. (Key A.)

1 Though faint, yet pursuing, we go on our way;
The Lord is our Leader, His word is our stay;
Though suffering, and sorrow, and trial be near,
The Lord is our Refuge, and whom can we fear?

2 He raiseth the fallen, He cheereth the faint;
The weak and oppress'd, He will hear their complaint;
The way may be weary, and thorny the road,
But how can we falter? our help is in God.

3 And to His green pastures our footsteps He leads;
His flock in the desert how kindly He feeds!
The lambs in His bosom He tenderly bears,
And brings back the wanderers all safe from the snares.

4 Though clouds may surround us, our God is our Light;
Though storms rage around us, our God is our Might;
So faint, yet pursuing, still onward we come;
The Lord is our Leader, and heaven is our home.

BLESSED ARE THE PURE IN HEART.

2 When the sun begins to rise,
  Spreading brightness through the skies,
  They will love to praise and bless
  Christ the Son of Righteousness.
  In the watches of the night,
  When the stars are clear and bright,
  "Thus the just shall shine" they say,
  "In the Resurrection day."

3 When the leaves in autumn die,
  Falling fast and silently,
  "These," they think, "that now seem dead,
  Shall in spring lift up their head."
  God in every thing they see:
  First in all their thoughts is He:
  They have loved the better part;
  Blessèd are the pure in heart! AMEN.

94. IN HEAVENLY LOVE ABIDING.

Mrs. Waring.   A. J. H.

1. In heav'n-ly love a-bid-ing, No change my heart shall fear, And safe is such con-fid-ing, For noth-ing chang-es here: The storm may roar with-out me, My heart may low be laid, But God is round a-bout me, And can I be dis-mayed?
2. Wher-ev-er He may guide me, No want shall turn me back; My Shep-herd is be-side me, And noth-ing can I lack: His wis-dom ev-er wak-eth; His sight is nev-er dim; He knows the way He tak-eth, And I will walk with Him.
3. Green pas-tures are be-fore me, Which yet I have not seen; Bright skies will soon be o'er me, Where dark-est clouds have been: My hope I can-not meas-ure; My path to life is free: My Sav-iour has my treas-ure, And He will walk with me.

ONWARD SPEED THY CONQUERING FLIGHT.

3 Onward speed thy conquering flight;
Angel, onward fly:
Long has been the reign of night;
Bring the morning nigh:
'T is to thee the heathen lift
Their imploring wail;
Bear them Heaven's holy gift,
Ere their courage fail.

4 Onward speed thy conquering flight;
Angel, onward speed;
Morning burst upon our sight—
'T is the time decreed:
Jesus now His kingdom takes,
Thrones and empires fall,
And the joyous song awakes,
"God is all in all."

PRAISE TO JESUS, LORD AND GOD.

W. Ball.   E. J. Hopkins.

1. Praise to Jesus, Lord and God, For the love He sheds a-broad, Light-ing o'er a world of sin, Glow-ing in the heart with-in; For the sa-cred stand-ard spread, For the life our Pat-tern led, For His pre-cept, pure and true, For His doc-trine, like the dew. A-MEN.

2 For His love's inviting call,
All embracing, seeking all,
For the grace and truth He brought;
For the ransom He hath wrought;
For the crown of thorns He wore;
For the painful cross He bore;
For the dying words He said;
For the blood of sprinkling shed:

3 For His glorious reign on high,
When He rose from Bethany;
For the heavenly peace He leaves;
For the blessings which He gives;
For the pledge that we shall rise,
In His likeness to the skies;
For the merciful decree
That our Friend our Judge shall be.

WEBB. (Key B Flat.)

1 I know no life divided,
   O Lord of Life, from Thee;
In Thee is life provided
For all mankind, for me:
I know no death, O Jesus,
   Because I live in Thee;
Thy death it is which frees us
From sin eternally.

2 I fear no tribulation,
   Since, whatsoe'er it be,
It makes no separation
Between my Lord and me:
If Thou, my God, my Teacher,
   Vouchsafe to be my own,
Though poor, I shall be richer
Than monarch on his throne.

3 Oh, hold Thou up my goings,
   And lead from strength to strength,
That unto Thee in Zion
I may appear at length:
Oh, make my spirit worthy
   To join that ransomed throng;
Oh, teach my lips to utter
That everlasting song.

4 Oh, give that last, best blessing
   That even saints can know,
To follow in Thy footsteps
Wherever Thou dost go.
Not wisdom, might, or glory,
   I ask to win above;
I ask for Thee, Thee only,
O Thou Eternal Love!

BETHANY. (Key G.)

1 Nearer, my God, to Thee,
   Nearer to Thee!
Even though it be a cross
   That raiseth me,
Still all my song shall be,
Nearer, my God, to Thee,
   Nearer to Thee!

2 Though like the wanderer,
   The sun goes down,
Darkness be over me,
   My rest a stone;
Yet in my dreams I'd be
Nearer, my God, to Thee,
   Nearer to Thee!

3 There let the way appear
   Steps unto heaven;
All that Thou sendest me,
   In mercy given:
Angels to beckon me,
Nearer, my God, to Thee,
   Nearer to Thee!

4 Then with my waking thoughts
   Bright with Thy praise,
Out of my stony griefs
   Bethel I'll raise:
So by my woes to be
Nearer, my God, to Thee,
   Nearer to Thee!

5 Or if on joyful wing
   Cleaving the sky,
Sun, moon, and stars forgot,
   Upward I fly,
Still all my song shall be,
Nearer, my God, to Thee,
   Nearer to Thee.

LITTLE TEMPLES.

1. Je-sus, can a child like me Thine own liv-ing tem-ple be?
Yes, Thy Spir-it day by day, In my heart will deign to stay;
Then my heart must ev-er be A fit dwell-ing place for Thee;
E-vil tem-per, thoughts of sin,— These things must not en-ter in.

2 But a temple is a place
Built for constant prayer and praise,
And the teaching of Thy word:
Am I such a temple, Lord?
Yes, if all I do and say,
In my work and in my play,
Shall be gentle, true, and right,
Pleasing in Thy holy sight.

3 Keep me, Lord, for I am weak;
Make me hear when Thou dost speak;
Cleanse my heart from every sin,
Make me beautiful within.
May Thy presence from above,
Fill my heart with holy love;
Then shall all about me see
That the Saviour dwells in me.

CREATION'S PRAISE.

2 Give glory to the Lord,
 Ye kindreds of the earth;
His sovereign power record,
 And show His wonders forth,
Till heathen tongues His grace proclaim,
And every heart adores His name.

3 'T is He the mountains crowns
 With forests waving wide;
'T is He old ocean bounds,
 And heaves her roaring tide;
He swells the tempests on the main,
Or breathes the zephyr o'er the plain.

4 Still let the waters roar,
 As around the earth they roll;
His praise forever more
 They sound from pole to pole.
'T is nature's wild, unconscious song
O'er thousand waves that floats along.

5 His praise, ye worlds on high,
 Display with all your spheres,
Amid the darksome sky,
 When silent night appears.
Oh, let His works declare His name
Through all the universal frame.

THE BEAUTY OF YOUTHFUL HOLINESS.

Miss E. M. Cogswell.   A. J. H.

1. When in shad-ow dark, a flow-er Faint-ly shows its form and hue,
But the sun-beam's won-drous pow-er Brings its beau-ty all to view:
So to childhood there are giv-en Charms which make it al-ways fair,
But the light of Christ from heav-en Adds a beau-ty, pure and rare.

2 Children's lips are dearest, saying
  Cheerful, tender words of love,
And their voices sweetest, praying
  To their Father dear, above.
Dimpled hands are pretty, playing,
  But are doubly dear and fair,
When the Lord's command obeying,
  "One another's burdens bear."

3 Children, tender love applying,
  Many wrongs can set aright;
Tears of sorrow sweetly drying,
  Making heavy hearts feel light.
Christ makes bright the path of duty;
  Walk ye in it, children dear,
And to life a richer beauty
  Shall be added year by year.

TRUST IN GOD.

2 God will never leave us,
  All our woes He knows,
Feels the pains that grieve us.
  Sees our care and woes :
When in grief we languish,
  He will dry the tear
Who His children's anguish
  Heals with comfort near.

3 All our woe and sadness
  In this world below
Lost will be in gladness :
  We in heaven shall know
When our gracious Saviour
  In His realms above
Welcomes us with favor,
  Crowns us with His love.

LOVE DIVINE, ALL LOVE EXCELLING.

1. Love divine, all love excelling, Joy of heaven to earth come down, Fix in us Thy humble dwelling, All Thy faithful mercies crown. Father, Thou art all compassion; Pure, unbounded love Thou art; Visit us with Thy salvation; Enter ev'ry longing heart.

2. Breathe, oh breathe Thy loving Spirit Into ev'ry troubled breast, Let us all Thy grace inherit, Let us find Thy promised rest; Take away the love of sinning, Take our load of guilt away; End the work of Thy beginning, Bring us to eternal day.

3 Come, almighty to deliver,
  Let us all Thy life receive;
  Suddenly return, and never,
    Never more Thy temples leave;
  Thee we would be always blessing,
    Serve Thee as thy hosts above,
  Pray, and praise Thee without ceasing,
    Glory in Thy perfect love.

4 Finish, then, Thy new creation;
  Pure and spotless may we be;
  Let us see our whole salvation,
    Perfectly secured by Thee,
  Changed from glory into glory,
    Till in heaven we take our place,
  Till we cast our crowns before Thee,
    Lost in wonder, love, and praise.

CHILDS. (Key A Flat.)

1 The thing my God doth hate,
　That I no more may do;
　Thy creature, Lord, again create,
　And all my soul renew:

2 My soul shall then, like Thine,
　Abhor the thing unclean,
　And, sanctified by love divine,
　Forever cease from sin.

3 That blessed law of Thine,
　Jesus, to me impart;
　The Spirit's law of life divine,
　Oh, write it on my heart!

4 Implant it deep within,
　Whence it may ne'er remove,—
　The law of liberty from sin,
　The perfect law of love.

5 Thy nature be my law,—
　Thy spotless sanctity;
　And sweetly every moment draw
　My happy soul to Thee.

6 Soul of my soul, remain!
　Who didst for all fulfil,
　In me, O Lord, fulfil again
　Thy heavenly Father's will.

HADDAM. (Key D.)

1 O Zion, tune thy voice,
　And raise thy hands on high;
　Tell all the earth thy joys,
　And boast salvation nigh:
　Cheerful in God, | While rays divine
　Arise and shine, | Stream all abroad.

2 He gilds thy mourning face
　With beams that cannot fade;
　His all-resplendent grace
　He pours around thy head:
　The nations round | With lustre new
　Thy form shall view, | Divinely crowned.

3 In honor to His name,
　Reflect that sacred light,
　And loud that grace proclaim
　Which makes thy darkness bright:
　Pursue His Praise, | In worlds above
　Till sovereign love | Thy Glory raise.

4 There, on His holy hill,
　A brighter Sun shall rise,
　And with His radiance fill
　Those fairer, purer skies:
　While round His throne | In nobler spheres
　Ten thousand stars | His influence own

MANOAH. (Key B Flat.)

1 Oh help us, Lord! each hour of need
　Thy heavenly succor give;
　Help us in thought, and word, and deed,
　Each hour on earth we live.

2 Oh help us, when our spirits bleed,
　With contrite anguish sore;
　And when our hearts are cold and dead,
　Oh help us, Lord, the more.

3 Oh help us through the prayer of faith
　More firmly to believe;
　For still the more the servant hath,
　The more shall he receive.

4 Oh help us, Father! from on high;
　We know no help but Thee;
　Oh! help us so to live and die,
　As Thine in heaven to be.

WHEN, HIS SALVATION BRINGING.

2 And since the Lord retaineth
   His love for children still,
Though now as King He reigneth
   On Zion's heavenly hill,
We'll flock around His banner,
   Who sits upon the throne;
And cry aloud, "Hosanna
   To David's royal Son."

3 For should we fail proclaiming
   Our great Redeemer's praise,
The stones, our silence shaming,
   Might well hosanna raise.
But shall we only render
   The tribute of our words?
No! while our hearts are tender,
   They, too, shall be the Lord's.

THE COMING OF THE LORD.

1. He will come, per-haps, at morn-ing, When to sim-ply live is sweet, When the arm is strong, un-wea-ried By the noon-day toil and heat, When the un-dimm'd eye looks tear-less Up the shin-ing heights of life, And the ea-ger soul is pant-ing, Yearn-ing for some no-ble strife.

2. He will come, per-haps, at noon-tide, When the pulse of life throbs high, When the fruits of toil are rip-'ning, And the har-vest time is nigh; Then thro' all the full-orb'd splen-dor Of the sun's me-ri-dian blaze, There may shine the strange, new beau-ty Of the Lord's trans-fig-ured face;

3 Or it may be in the evening,—
Gray and sombre is the sky,
Clouds around the sunset gather,
Far and dark the shadows lie;
When we long for rest and slumber,
And some tender thoughts of home
Fill the heart with vague, sad yearning,
Then perhaps the Lord will come.

4 If He only finds us ready
In the morning's happy light,
In the strong and fiery noontide,
Or the coming of the night,—
If He only finds us waiting,
Listening for His sudden call,
Then His coming when we think not
Is the sweetest hope of all.

106   WAIT ON THE LORD.

S. L. Cuthbert.   A. J. H.

1. When clouds hang heav-y o'er thy way, And darker grows the weary day, And Thou oppressed with anxious care, Art almost tempted to despair, Still wait upon the Lord, Still wait upon the Lord.

2. When friends betray thy loving trust, And thou art humbled in the dust, When dearest joys from thee have fled, And Hope within Thy heart lies dead, Still wait upon the Lord, Still wait upon the Lord.

3 When death comes knocking at thy door
And in thy home are sorrows sore,
When age comes on, and eyes grow dim,
Still look to Christ, still trust in Him,
    (*Repeat*)—And wait upon the Lord.

4 Whate'er thy care, believe His word ;
In joy or grief trust in the Lord ;
Good courage He will give to thee,
And strong indeed thy heart shall be
    (*Repeat*)—By waiting on the Lord.

SUFFER THE LITTLE CHILDREN TO COME UNTO ME. 107

ESPECIALLY WRITTEN FOR THIS COLLECTION BY
MRS. C. M. SAWYER.

A. J. IL

1. How many things still dear to-day, The gentle Saviour used to say, When here upon the earth he walked, And with the people lived and talked! But, dearer none than this could be, "Suffer the little children to come unto me."

2. We were not born in Palestine,
Dear Lord, to hear those words of Thine;
We did not, on Thy loving breast
With all the happy children rest;
But we can read the tender plea,
"Suffer little children to come unto me."

3. We know Thy walks on earth are o'er;
The children find Thee here no more:
But where Thou art there is a place
For us where we shall see Thy face,
And hear the joyous words from Thee
"Suffer little children to come unto me."

BRIGHTLY GLEAMS OUR BANNER.

T. J. PORTER. HAYDN.

1. Brightly gleams our ban - ner, Point-ing to the sky, Wav-ing wanderers on - ward To their home on high. Jour-ney-ing o'er the des-ert, Glad-ly thus we pray, And with hearts u - nit - ed Take our heavenward way. Bright-ly gleams our ban - ner, Point-ing to the sky, Wav-ing wanderers on - ward To their home on high. A-MEN.

2. Je - sus, Lord and Mas - ter, At Thy sa - cred feet, Here with hearts re- joic - ing See Thy chil - dren meet; Oft - en have we left Thee, Oft-en gone a - stray, Keep us, might-y Sav- iour, In the nar- row way. Bright-ly gleams our ban - ner,

3 All our days direct us
In the way we go,
Lead us on victorious
Over every foe;
Bid Thine angels shield us
When the storm-clouds lower,
Pardon, Thou, and save us
In the last dread hour.
Brightly gleams, &c.

4 Then with saints and angels
May we join above,
Offering prayers and praises
At Thy throne of love;
When the toil is over,
Then comes rest and peace,
Jesus, in His beauty,
Songs that never cease.
Brightly gleams, &c.

BRATTLE STREET. (Key D.)

1 While Thee I seek, protecting power,
   Be my vain wishes stilled;
And may this consecrated hour
   With better hopes be filled.
Thy love the power of tho't bestowed;
   To Thee my thoughts would soar;
Thy mercy o'er my life has flowed;
   That mercy I adore.

2 In each event of life, how clear
   Thy ruling hand I see!
Each blessing to my soul more dear,
   Because conferred by Thee.
In every joy that crowns my days
   In every pain I bear,
My heart shall find delight in praise,
   Or seek relief in prayer.

3 When gladness wings my favored hour,
   Thy love my thoughts shall fill;
Resigned, when storms of sorrow lower,
   My soul shall meet Thy will.
My lifted eye, without a tear,
   The gathering storm shall see:
My steadfast heart shall know no fear;
   That heart shall rest on Thee.

SWEET HOUR OF PRAYER. (Key D.)

1 Sweet hour of prayer! sweet hour of prayer!
   That calls me from a world of care,
And bids me at my Father's throne,
   Make all my wants and wishes known:
In seasons of distress and grief,
   My soul has often found relief;
‖: And oft escaped the tempter's snare
   By thy return, sweet hour of prayer.:‖

2 Sweet hour of prayer! sweet hour of prayer!
   Thy wings shall my petition bear,
To Him whose truth and faithfulness,
   Engage the waiting soul to bless;
And since He bids me seek His face,
   Believe His word and trust His grace,
‖: I'll cast on Him my every care,
   And wait for thee, sweet hour of prayer.:‖

3 Sweet hour of prayer! sweet hour of prayer!
   May I thy consolation share:
Till from true faith's commanding height,
   I view my home, and take my flight:
This robe of flesh I'll drop, and rise
   To seize the everlasting prize;
‖: And shout, while passing through the air,
   Farewell, farewell, sweet hour of prayer!:‖

FEDERAL STREET. (Key A Flat.)

1 O God, Thou art my God alone;
   Early to Thee my soul shall cry,
A pilgrim in a land unknown,
   A thirsty land whose springs are dry.

2 Yet through this rough and thorny maze
   I follow hard on Thee, my God;
Thy hand unseen upholds my ways;
   I safely tread where Thou hast trod.

3 Thee, in the watches of the night,
   When I remember on my bed,
Thy presence makes the darkness light;
   Thy guardian wings are round my head.

4 Better than life itself Thy love,
   Dearer than all beside to me;
For whom have I in heaven above,
   Or what on earth compared with Thee!

ANNIVERSARY HYMN.

Wm. H. Harden. A. J. H.

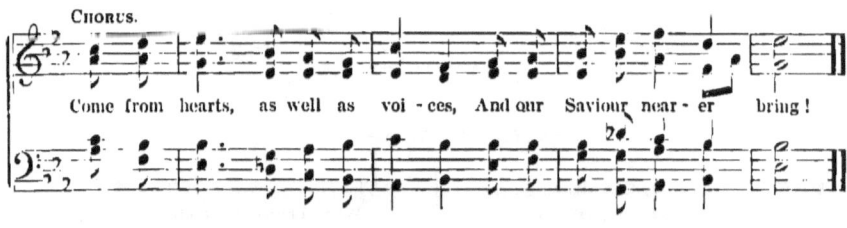

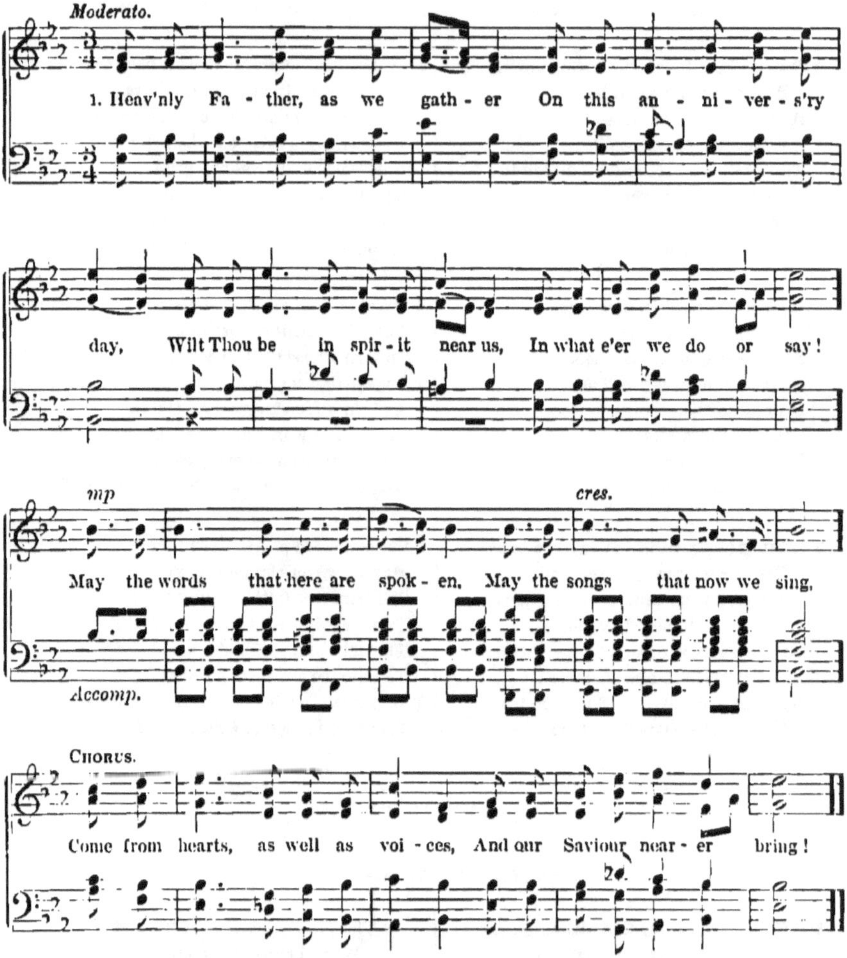

2 Days and years, gone by, will never,
Never more to us return;
May we make the present blessed,
And of Jesus meekly learn!
Clothe us all in lowly spirit,
Make us humble, pure, sincere;
In the day of joy, surround us,
In the hour of sorrow, cheer.

3 Speeding onward towards the future,
Leaving present things behind,
May we learn the heav'nly lesson,
To be true and to be kind;
True to God and to our Saviour,
Kind in all our acts and ways;
Give of charity full measure,
And to Thee, through Christ, the praise!

GLORIOUS THINGS OF THEE ARE SPOKEN.

J. Newton.
Arr. from S. Smith.

2 See, the streams of living waters
  Springing from eternal love,
Still supp'y Thy sons and daughters,
  And a'l fear of want remove.
Who can faint while such a river
  Ever flows our thirst t' assuage!
Grace, which, like the Lord, the giver,
  Never fails from age to age.

3 Round each habitation hovering,
  See the cloud and fire appear;
For a glory and a covering,
  Showing that the Lord is near:
He who gives us daily manna,
  He who listens when we cry,
Let Him hear the loud hosanna
  Rising to His throne on high.

BANNOCKBURN.

Rev. A. C. Thomas.  Scottish Melody.

1. Thou whose wide extend-ed sway Suns and sys-tems e'er o-bey: Thou our Guard-ian and our Stay, Ev-er more adored: In prospec-tive, Lord, we see Jew and Gentile, bond and free, Re-con-ciled in Christ to Thee, Ho-ly, ho-ly Lord.

2 Thou by all shalt be confessed,
Ever blessing, ever blest,
When, to Thy eternal rest,
　In the courts above,
Thou shalt bring the sore oppressed,
Fill each joy-desiring breast,
Make of each a welcome guest,
　At the feast of love.

3 When destroying death shall die,
Hushed be every rising sigh,
Tears be wiped from every eye,
　Never more to fall;
Then shall praises fill the sky,
And angelic hosts shall cry,
Holy, Holy, Lord Most High,
　Thou art all in all!

(SECOND HYMN.)
WE NEVER PART FROM THEE.

1 God who dwellest everywhere,
God who makest all Thy care,
God who hearest every prayer,
　Thou who seest the heart,—
Thou to whom we lift our eyes,
Father, help our souls to rise,
And beyond these narrow skies
　See Thee as Thou art.

2 Let our anxious thought be still,
Holy trust adore Thy will,
Holy love our bosoms fill;
　Let our songs ascend,
Dearest friends may parted be
All our earthly treasures flee,
Yet we never part from Thee,
　Our Eternal Friend.
　　　　Eliza Lee Follen.

TOPLADY. (Key B Flat.)

1 Rock of Ages, cleft for me,
   Let me hide myself in Thee;
   Let the water and the blood,
   From Thy side a healing flood,
   Be of sin the double cure,
   Cleanse me from its guilt and power.

2 Not the labors of my hands
   Can fulfil Thy law's demands;
   Could my zeal no respite know,
   Could my tears forever flow,
   All for sin could not atone;
   Thou canst save, and Thou alone.

3 Nothing in my hand I bring;
   Simply to Thy cross I cling;
   Naked, come to Thee for dress:
   Helpless, look to Thee for grace;
   Foul, I to the Fountain fly:
   Wash me, Saviour, or I die!

4 While I draw this fleeting breath,
   When my eyelids close in death,
   When I rise to worlds unknown,
   And behold Thee on Thy throne,
   Rock of Ages, cleft for me,
   Let me hide myself in Thee.

HEBRON. (Key B Flat.)

1 Blest hour! when mortal man retires
   To hold communion with His God,
   To send to heaven his warm desires,
   And listen to the sacred word.

2 Blest hour! when God Himself draws nigh,
   Well pleased His people's voice to hear,
   To hush the penitential sigh,
   And wipe away the mourner's tear.

3 Blest hour! for where the Lord resorts
   Foretastes of future bliss are given,
   And mortals find His earthly courts
   The house of God, the gate of heaven.

4 Hail, peaceful hour! supremely blest
   Amid the hours of worldly care,
   The hour that yields the spirit rest,
   That sacred hour, the hour of prayer.

5 And when my hours of prayer are past,
   And this frail tenement decays,
   Then may I spend in heaven at last
   A never-ending hour of praise.

NETTLETON. (Key E.)

1 Saviour, breathe an evening blessing,
   Ere repose our spirits seal;
   Sin and want we come confessing;
   Thou canst save and Thou canst heal.

2 Though destruction walk around us,
   Though the arrows past us fly,
   Angel guards from Thee surround us;
   We are safe, if Thou art nigh.

3 Though the night be dark and dreary,
   Darkness cannot hide from Thee;
   Thou art He who, never weary,
   Watchest where Thy people be.

4 Should swift death this night o'ertake us,
   And command us to the tomb,
   May the morn in heaven awake us,
   Clad in bright, eternal bloom.

3 There is the throne of David;
And there, from care released,
The shout of them that triumph,
The song of them that feast.
And they, who with their Leader,
Have conquered in the fight,
For ever and for ever
Are clad in robes of white.

4 O sweet and blessèd country,
The home of God's elect!
O sweet and blessèd country,
That eager hearts expect!
Jesus, in mercy bring us
To that dear land of rest,
Who art, with God the Father
And Spirit, ever blest.

SOMETIMES A LIGHT SURPRISES.

115

COWPER. S. THALBERG.

3 It can bring with it nothing,
   But He will bear us through;
   Who gives the lilies clothing,
   Will clothe His people too:
   Beneath the spreading heavens,
   No creature but is fed;
   And He who feeds the ravens,
   Will give His children bread.

4 Though vine, nor fig tree neither,
   Its wonted fruit should bear;
   Though all the field should wither,
   Nor flocks, nor herds be there;
   Yet God the same abiding,
   His praise shall tune my voice;
   For while in Him confiding
   I cannot but rejoice.

GOD IS LOVE.

A. J. H.

1. God is love; His mer-cy bright-ens All the paths in which we rove;
Bliss He wakes, and woe He light-ens; God is wis-dom, God is love.

2. Chance and change are bus-y ev-er; Man de-cays and a-ges move;
But His mer-cy wan-eth nev-er; God is wis-dom, God is love.

3 E'en the hour that darkest seemeth
Will His changeless goodness prove;
From the gloom His brightness streameth;
God is wisdom, God is love.

4 He with earthly cares entwineth
Hope and comfort from above:
Everywhere His glory shineth;
God is wisdom, God is love.

THE WILDBIRD'S LESSON.

Mrs. C. M. Sawyer. A. J. H.

1. The birds that speed their fear-less flight, When northern hills grow bleak, To lands whose skies are al-ways bright, A warm-er home to seek;

2 With tireless wing and steady eye
Their journey still pursue,
For God, along the stormiest sky,
Conducts them safely through.

3 Oh, if the wildbird keeps the way
Thus marked by God for her,
Nor starless night nor sunless day
Can lead her flight to err—

4 Shall we, around whose restless feet
A light diviner falls,
Like blind men wand'ring in the street,
Turn where each tempter calls?

5 No, Father, no! Or if our soul
Perchance awhile should stray,
The wildbird winging to its goal
Shall teach the better way.

LISBON. (Key B Flat.)

1 WELCOME, sweet day of rest
    That saw the Lord arise !
  Welcome to this reviving breast,
    And these rejoicing eyes !

2 The King Himself comes near,
    And feasts His saints to-day ;
  Here may we sit and see Him here,
    And love, and praise, and pray.

3 One day amidst the place
    Where my dear God hath been,
  Is sweeter than ten thousand days
    Of pleasurable sin.

4 My willing soul would stay
    In such a frame as this,
  And sit and sing herself away
    To everlasting bliss.

DENNIS. (Key G.)

1 FOR all Thy saints, O Lord,
    Who strove in Thee to live,
  Who followed Thee, obeyed, adored,
    Our grateful hymn receive.

2 For all Thy saints, O Lord,
    Accept our thankful cry,
  Who counted Thee their great reward,
    And strove in Thee to die.

3 They all, in life or death,
    With Thee, their Lord, in view,
  Learned from Thy Holy Spirit's breath
    To suffer and to do.

4 For this, Thy name we bless,
    And humbly pray that we
  May follow them in holiness,
    And live and die in Thee.

HENDON. (Key G.)

1 THEY who seek the throne of grace
  Find that throne in every place ;
  If we live a life of prayer,
  God is present everywhere.

2 In our sickness and our health,
  In our want, or in our wealth,
  If we look to God in prayer,
  God is present everywhere.

3 When our earthly comforts fail,
  When the woes of life prevail,
  'T is the time for earnest prayer ;
  God is present everywhere.

4 Then, my soul, in every strait,
  To thy Father come, and wait ;
  He will answer every prayer :
  God is present everywhere.

ARMENIA. (Key A Flat.)

1 As pants the hart for cooling streams,
    When heated in the chase,
  So longs my soul, O God, for Thee,
    And Thy refreshing grace.

2 For Thee, my God, the living God,
    My thirsty soul doth pine ;
  Oh, when shall I behold Thy face,
    Thou Majesty Divine ?

3 Why restless, why cast down, my soul ?
    Trust God, and He'll employ
  His aid for thee, and change these sighs
    To thankful hymns of joy.

4 Why restless, why cast down, my soul ?
    Hope still, and Thou shalt sing
  The praise of Him who is Thy God,
    Thy health's eternal Spring.

JESUS CHRIST, OUR SAVIOUR.

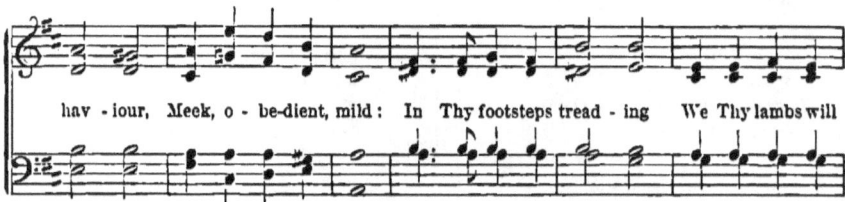

2 For the varied blessings
  Given us to share ;
Mother's fond caressings,
  Father's guardian care ;
For our friends and kindred,
  For our daily food,
For our wanderings hindered,
  For our learning good.

3 For all Thou bestowest,
  All Thou dost withhold ;
Whatsoe'er Thou knowest
  Best for us, Thy fold ;
For all gifts and graces
  While we live below,
Till in heavenly places
  We Thy face shall know.

4 We, Thy children, raising
  Unto Thee our hearts,
In Thy constant praising
  Bear our duteous parts.
As Thy love hath won us
  From the world away,
Still Thy hands put on us ;
  Bless us day by day.

5 Let Thine angels guide us ;
  Let Thine arms enfold ;
In Thy bosom hide us,
  Sheltered from the cold ;
To Thyself us gather,
  With the blessed throng,
There to join forever
  In the heav'nly song. AMEN.

LEAD, KINDLY LIGHT.

Rev. J. B. Dykes.

2 I was not ever thus, nor pray'd that Thou
   Shouldst lead me on;
I loved to choose and see my path; but now
   Lead Thou me on.
I loved the garish day: and, spite of fears,
Pride ruled my will; remember not past years.

3 So long Thy power has blest me, sure it still
   Will lead me on
O'er moor and fen, o'er crag and torrent, till
   The night is gone.
And with the morn those angel faces smile,
Which I have loved long since, and lost awhile.
                                        Amen.

120. THE FATHER'S CALL.

Mrs. C. M. Sawyer.   "MY SON, GIVE ME THY HEART."   A. J. H.

1. Give me thy heart, My child, while youth Still scatters flow'rs a-round thy way; Oh, early seek the ways of truth, Lest evil tempt thy feet to stray.

2. Come un-to Me! The yoke I lay Up-on thy youth-ful neck is light: My bur-den grows from day to day, More dear to sense, more fair to sight.

3 Come unto Me! The crown I press
  Upon thy brow hath not a thorn;
  A crown so rare to soothe and bless,
  No royal head hath ever worn.

4 Come to Me now! This hour decide
  Through all the years Mine own to be;
  Oh, for His sake who for thee died,
  My wandering child, come home to Me!

THE LORD IS MY SHEPHERD.

2. Thro' the valley and shadow of death tho' I stray,
Since Thou art my Guardian, no evil I fear;
Thy rod shall defend me, Thy staff be my stay;
No harm can befall, with my Comforter near.

3. Let goodness and mercy, my bountiful God,
Still follow my steps till I meet Thee above;
I seek, by the path which my forefathers trod
Thro' the land of their sojourn, Thy kingdom of love.

MY SHEPHERD.

Author unknown.   A. J. H.

1. "He leadeth me!" And so I need not seek My own wild way A-cross the desert wild; He knoweth where the soft, green pastures lie, Where the still waters glide, ... And how to reach the coolness of their rest Beneath the calm hillside.

2 "He leadeth me!"
And though it be by rugged, weary ways
Where thorns spring sharp and sore,
No pathway can seem strange or desolate
Where Jesus goes before.
His gentle shepherding my solace is,
And gladness yet in store.

3 "He leadeth me!"
I shall not take one needless step through all,
In wind or heat or cold;
And all day long He sees the peaceful end
Through trials manifold.
Up the fair hillside, like some sweet surprise
Waiteth the quiet fold.

MERIBAH. (Key E Flat.)

1 AUTHOR of faith, to Thee we cry,
　To Thee, who wouldst not have us die,
But know the truth and live;
Open our eyes to see Thy face;
Work in our hearts the saving grace;
　The life eternal give.

2 Shut up in unbelief, we groan,
And blindly serve a God unknown,
　Till Thou the veil remove;
The gift unspeakable impart,
And write Thy name upon my heart,
　And manifest Thy love.

3 We know the work is only Thine;
The gift of faith is all divine;
　But, if on Thee we call,
Thou wilt that gracious gift bestow,
And cause our hearts to feel and know
　That Thou hast died for all.

4 Thou bidst us knock and enter in,
Come unto Thee, and rest from sin,
　The blessing seek and find;
Thou bidst us ask Thy grace, and have;
Thou canst, Thou wouldst, this moment save
　Both me and all mankind.

5 Be it according to Thy word;
Now let us find our pard'ning Lord;
　Let what we ask be given:
The bar of unbelief remove:
Open the door of faith and love,
　And lead us into heaven.

MARTYN. (Key F.)

1 JESUS, lover of my soul,
　Let me to Thy bosom fly,
While the nearer waters roll,
　While the tempest still is high;
Hide me, O my Saviour, hide,
　Till the storm of life is past;
Safe into the haven guide,
　Oh, receive my soul at last.

2 Other refuge have I none;
　Hangs my helpless soul on Thee;
Leave, oh, leave me not alone!
　Still support and comfort me:
All my trust on Thee is stay'd;
　All my help from Thee I bring;
Cover my defenceless head
　With the shadow of Thy wing.

3 Thou, O Christ, art all I want;
　More than all in Thee I find;
Raise the fallen, cheer the faint,
　Heal the sick, and lead the blind
Just and holy is Thy name:
　I am all unrighteousness;
False, and full of sin I am;
　Thou art full of truth and grace.

4 Plenteous grace with Thee is found,
　Grace to cover all my sin;
Let the healing streams abound;
　Make and keep me pure within.
Thou of life the Fountain art;
　Freely let me take of Thee:
Spring Thou up within my heart;
　Rise to all eternity.

SOLITUDE. (Key F.)

1 SOFTLY now the light of day
　Fades upon my sight away;
Free from care, from labor free,
　Lord, I would commune with Thee!

2 Thou, whose all pervading eye
　Nought escapes without, within,

Pardon each infirmity,
　Open fault, and secret sin!

3 Soon, for me, the light of day
　Shall forever pass away;
Then, from sin and sorrow free
　Take me, Lord, to dwell with Thee!

2 Clearer, still, and clearer
   Dawns the light from heaven,
In our sadness bringing
   News of sins forgiven.
Life has lost its shadows,
   Pure the light within;
Thou hast shed Thy radiance
   On a world of sin.

3 Brighter still and brighter
   Glows the western sun,
Shedding all its gladness
   O'er our work that's done.
Time will soon be over,
   Toil and sorrow past;
May we, blessed Saviour,
   Find a rest at last.

ANGEL VOICES EVER SINGING.

F. Pott.
Arthur S. Sullivan.

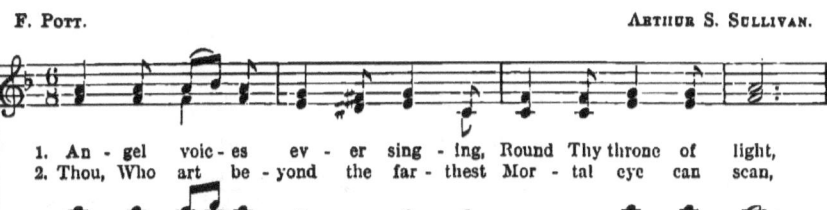

1. An-gel voic-es ev-er sing-ing, Round Thy throne of light,
2. Thou, Who art be-yond the far-thest Mor-tal eye can scan,

An-gel harps for-ev-er ring-ing, Rest not day nor night;
Can it be that Thou re-gard-est Songs of sin-ful man?

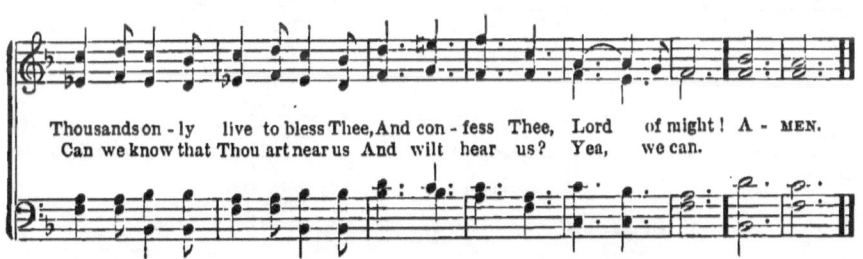

Thousands on-ly live to bless Thee, And con-fess Thee, Lord of might! A - MEN.
Can we know that Thou art near us And wilt hear us? Yea, we can.

3 Yea, we know that Thou rejoicest
   O'er each work of Thine;
Thou didst ears, and hands, and voices,
   For thy praise combine;
Craftman's art and music's measure
   For Thy pleasure,
     Didst design.

4 In Thy house great God we offer
   Of Thine own to Thee
And for thine acceptance proffer
   All unworthily
Hearts and minds and hands and voices,
   In our choicest
     Melody.

WHEN SHALL THE VOICE OF SINGING.

J. EDMESTON.   ARR. FROM SCHUMANN.

2 Then from the craggy mountains
   The sacred shout shall fly,
And shady vales and fountains
   Shall echo the reply;
High tower and lowly dwelling
   Shall send the chorus round,
The hallelujah swelling
   In one eternal sound.

DOWNS. (Key E.)

1 O God, we praise Thee, and confess
   That Thou, the only Lord
   And everlasting Father, art
   By all the earth adored.

2 To Thee all angels cry aloud,
   To Thee the powers on high,
   Both cherubim and seraphim,
   Continually do cry,

3 "O holy, holy, holy Lord,
   Whom heavenly hosts obey,
   The world is with the glory filled
   Of Thy majestic sway."

4 Th' apostles' glorious company,
   And prophets, crowned with light,
   With all the martyrs' noble host,
   Thy constant praise recite.

5 The holy church throughout the world,
   O Lord, confesses Thee,—
   That Thou eternal Father art
   Of boundless majesty.

BALERMA. (Key B Flat.)

1 On happy soul that lives on high
   While men lie grovelling here!
   His hopes are fixed above the sky,
   And faith forbids his fear.

2 His conscience knows no secret stings,
   While peace and joy combine
   To form a life whose holy springs
   Are hidden and divine.

3 He waits in secret on his God;
   His God in secret sees:
   Let earth be all in arms abroad,
   He dwells in heavenly peace.

4 His pleasures rise from things unseen,
   Beyond this world of time,
   Where neither eyes nor ears have been,
   Nor thoughts of mortals climb.

5 He wants no pomp nor royal throne
   To raise his honor here,
   Content and pleased to live unknown
   Till Christ, his Life, appear.

YOAKLEY. (Key E.)

1 THE Lord my pasture shall prepare,
   And feed me with a shepherd's care;
   His presence shall my wants supply,
   And guard me with a watchful eye:
   My noon-day walks He shall attend,
   And all my midnight hours defend.

2 When in the sultry glebe I faint,
   Or on the thirsty mountain pant,
   To fertile vales and dewy meads,
   My weary, wand'ring steps He leads,
   Where peaceful rivers, soft and slow,
   Amid the verdant landscape flow.

3 Though in a bare and rugged way,
   Through devious, lonely wilds I stray,
   Thy bounty shall my pains beguile,
   The barren wilderness shall smile,
   With sudden greens and herbage crown'd,
   And streams shall murmur all around.

4 Though in the paths of death I tread,
   With gloomy horrors overspread,
   My steadfast heart shall fear no ill,
   For Thou, O Lord, art with me still:
   Thy friendly crook shall give me aid,
   And guide me through the dreadful shade.

128   I HEARD THE VOICE OF JESUS SAY.

H. Bonar.   J. F. Reichardt, 1781.

1. I heard the voice of Jesus say, Come unto me and rest; Lay down thou weary one, lay down Thy head upon my breast. I came to Jesus as I was, Weary and worn and sad, I found in Him a resting place, And He has made me glad.

2 I heard the voice of Jesus say,
  Behold I freely give
The living water; thirsty one,
  Stoop down, and drink, and live.
I came to Jesus, and I drank
  Of that life-giving stream;
My thirst was quenched, my soul revived,
  And now I live in Him.

3 I heard the voice of Jesus say,
  I am this dark world's light;
Look unto me, thy morn shall rise,
  And all thy day be bright.
I looked to Jesus, and I found
  In Him my Star, my Sun;
And in that light of life I'll walk,
  'Till travelling days are done.

THE GOSPEL BANNER.

2 Yes, Thou shalt reign forever,
  O Jesus, King of kings!
Thy light, Thy love, Thy favor,
  Each ransomed captive sings.
The isles for Thee are waiting,
  The deserts learn Thy praise,
The hills and valleys greeting,
  The song responsive raise.

GOD IS MY STRONG SALVATION.

2 Place on the Lord reliance;
My soul, with courage wait;
His truth be thine affiance,
When faint and desolate:
His might thine heart shall strengthen;
His love thy joy increase;
Mercy thy days shall lengthen;
The Lord will give thee peace.

THE TRIUMPH OF CHRIST.

2 Come, O ye kings, ye nations come,
   With songs of gladness hail Him;
   Ye gentiles all before Him fall,
     The royal Priest in Salem.
   O'er sin and death triumphantly
    Your conquering Lord hath risen;
   His praises sound Whose power hath bound
    Your ruthless foe in prison.

3 All hail, Thou King of glory, hail,
   Head of the new creation;
   Thy ways of grace we love to trace,
    And praise Thy great salvation.
   Thy heart was pressed with sorrow sore,
    The bonds of death to sever,
   To make us free that we might be
    Thy crown of joy forever.

132. PRAISE TO THEE, THOU GREAT CREATOR.

2 For ten thousand blessings given,
　For the hope of future joy,
Sound His praise through earth and heaven,
　Sound Jehovah's praise on high.
Joyfully on earth adore Him,
　Till in heaven our song we raise;
There, enraptured, fall before Him,
　Lost in wonder, love, and praise.

2 The dearest gift of Heaven,
   Love's written word of truth,
  To us is early given,
   To guide our steps in youth;
  We hear the wondrous story,
   The tale of Calvary;
  We read of homes in glory,
   From sin and sorrow free.

3 Redeemer, grant Thy blessing;
   Oh, teach us how to pray,
  That each, Thy fear possessing,
   May tread life's onward way;
  Then where the pure are dwelling
   We hope to meet again,
  And sweeter numbers swelling,
   Forever praise Thy name.

134 THE GATHERING PLACE.

AUTHOR UNKNOWN. CHARLES H. HOYT.

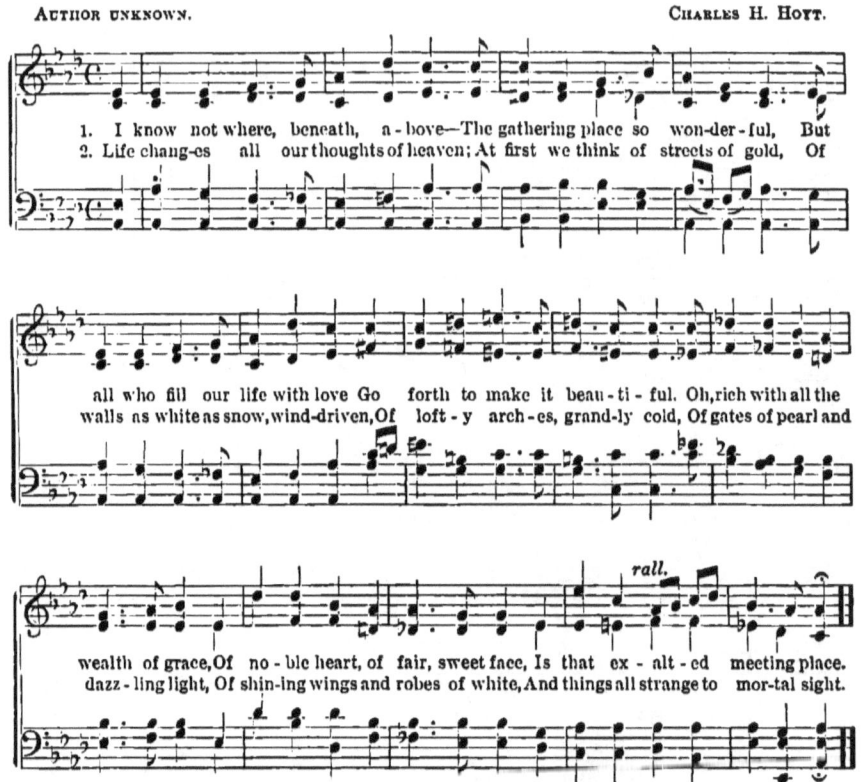

1. I know not where, beneath, a-bove—The gathering place so won-der-ful, But all who fill our life with love Go forth to make it beau-ti-ful. Oh, rich with all the wealth of grace, Of no-ble heart, of fair, sweet face, Is that ex-alt-ed meeting place.

2. Life chang-es all our thoughts of heaven; At first we think of streets of gold, Of walls as white as snow, wind-driven, Of loft-y arch-es, grand-ly cold, Of gates of pearl and dazz-ling light, Of shin-ing wings and robes of white, And things all strange to mor-tal sight.

3 But in the afterward of years
It is a more familiar place;
A home unhurt by sighs and tears,
Where waiteth many a well known face;
Where little children play and sing,
And maidens and the old men bring
Their tributes to the gracious King.

4 With passing months it comes more near,
It grows more real day by day;
Not strange or cold, but very dear,
The glad homeland not far away!
Where no sea toucheth, making moan,
Where none are poor, or sick, or lone,
The place where we shall find our own!

5 And as we think of all we knew,
Who there have met and part no more,
Our longing hearts desire home, too,
With all the strife and trouble o'er.
So poor the world, now they have gone
We scarcely dare to think upon
The years before our rest is won.

6 And yet our Father knoweth best
The joy or sadness that we need,
The time when we may take our rest,
And be from sin and sorrow freed.
So we will wait with patient grace,
Till in that blessed gathering place
We meet our friends and see His face.

HE HATH MADE ALL THINGS BEAUTIFUL.

Miss E. M. Cogswell.   Charles H. Hoyt.
Allegretto.

3 Sweetest music fills the air
  Waters murmuring soft and low,
  Joyous birds, with plumage rare,
    Singing praise where'er we go.
‖: Let our happy voices ring
    In the songs of praise we sing. :‖

4 But the dearest gifts of all
  Are the words and deeds of love,
  Smiles, that like the sunbeams fall,
    Hearts, with beauty from above :
‖: Let each life shed love's fair light ;
    Make the path to heaven more bright. :‖

136. THE HEAVENS DECLARE HIS GLORY.

2 There, from His bright pavilion,
   Like eastern bridegroom clad,
   Hailed by earth's thousand million,
   The sun sets forth ; right glad,
   His glorious race commencing,
   The mighty giant seems ;
   Through the vast round dispensing
   His all-pervading beams.

3 So pure, so soul-restoring
   Is truth's diviner ray !
   A brighter radiance pouring
   Than all the pomp of day :
   The wanderer surely guiding,
   It makes the simple wise ;
   And evermore abiding,
   Unfailing joy supplies.

OLD HUNDRED. (Key A.)

1 BE Thou, O God, exalted high;
And as Thy glory fills the sky,
So let it be on earth displayed,
Till Thou art here, as there, obeyed.

2 O God, our hearts are fixed and bent
Their thankful tribute to present;
And, with the heart, the voice, we'll raise
To Thee, our God, in songs of praise.

3 Thy praises, Lord, we will resound
To all the listening nations round;
Thy mercy highest heaven transcends;
Thy truth beyond the clouds extends.

4 Be Thou, O God, exalted high;
And as Thy glory fills the sky,
So let it be on earth displayed,
Till Thou art here, as there, obeyed.

PARK STREET. (Key A.)

1 WHEN Israel, of the Lord beloved,
Out from the land of bondage came,
Her father's God before her moved,
An awful guide, in smoke and flame.

2 By day, along the astonish'd lands
The cloudy pillar glided slow;
By night, Arabia's crimson'd sands
Return'd the fiery column's glow.

3 Thus present still, though now unseen,
When brightly shines the prosp'rous day,
Be thoughts of Thee a cloudy screen,
To temper the deceitful ray.

4 And, oh! when gathers on our path,
In shade and storm, the frequent night,
Be thou, long-suff'ring, slow to wrath,
A burning and a shining light.

NETTLETON. (Key E.)

1 COME, thou Fount of every blessing,
Tune my heart to sing Thy grace;
Streams of mercy never ceasing,
Call for songs of loudest praise.

2 Teach me some melodious sonnet,
Sung by flaming tongues above:
Praise, the mount—I'm fixed upon it—
Mount of God's unchanging love.

3 Oh! to grace how great a debtor
Daily I'm constrained to be!
Let that grace now, like a fetter,
Bind my wandering heart to Thee.

4 Prone to wander, Lord, I feel it—
Prone to leave the God I love—
Here's my heart—O take and seal it;
Seal it from Thy courts above.

TALLIS EVENING HYMN. (Key G.)

1 GLORY to Thee, my God, this night,
For all the blessings of the light:
Keep me, O, keep me, King of kings,
Beneath the shadow of Thy wings.

2 Forgive me, Lord, through Thy dear Son,
The ills which I this day have done;
That with the world, myself, and Thee,
I, ere I sleep, at peace may be.

3 O, may my soul on Thee repose,
And with sweet sleep mine eyelids close!
Sleep that shall me more vigorous make
To serve my God when I awake.

4 Lord, let my heart forever share
The bliss of Thy paternal care:
'Tis heaven on earth, 'tis heaven above,
To see Thy face and sing Thy love.

138. WE COME IN CHILDHOOD'S INNOCENCE.

Thomas Gray, Jr.
Alberto Randegger.

1. We come in childhood's in - no - cence, We come as chil - dren free; We of - fer up, O God, our hearts In trust - ing love to Thee. Well may we bend in sol - emn joy, At Thy bright courts a - bove; Well may a grate - ful child re - joice In such a Fa - ther's love.

2 We come not as the mighty come;
  Not as the proud we bow;
  But as the pure in heart should find,
  Seek we Thine altar now.
  "Forbid them not," the Saviour said :
  In speechless rapture dumb,
  We hear the call, we seek Thy face,
  Father, we come, we come.

2 Tender Shepherd, never leave us
   From Thy fold to go astray;
   By Thy look of love directed,
   May we walk the narrow way:
   Thus direct us, and protect us,
   Lest we fall to sin a prey.

3 Let Thy holy Word instruct us,
   Fill our minds with heavenly light;
   Let Thy love and grace constrain us
   To approve whate'er is right;
   Take Thine easy yoke, and wear it;
   Feel Thy heavy burden light.

3 While life's dark maze I tread,
And griefs around me spread,
Be Thou my Guide;
Bid darkness turn to day,
Wipe sorrow's tears away,
Nor let me ever stray
From Thee aside.

4 When ends life's transient dream,
When death's cold, sullen stream
Shall o'er me roll,
Blest Saviour, then, in love,
Fear and distrust remove;
Oh bear me safe above,
A ransomed soul.

TO THEE, MY GOD AND SAVIOUR.

HAWEIS. A. J. H.

2 Soon as the morn with roses
　Bedecks the dewy east,
And when the sun reposes
　Upon the ocean's breast,
My voice in supplication,
　Jehovah, Thou shalt hear:
Oh grant me Thy salvation,
　And to my soul draw near.

3 By Thee through life supported,
　I pass the dangerous road,
With heavenly hosts escorted
　Up to their bright abode;
There cast my crown before Thee,
　My toils and conflicts o'er,
And day and night adore Thee:
　What can an angel more?

142. IN THE CROSS OF CHRIST I GLORY.

2 When the sun of bliss is beaming
Light and love upon my way,
From the cross the radiance streaming
Adds new lustre to the day.
Bane and blessing, pain and pleasure,
By the cross are sanctified;
Peace is there that knows no measure,
Joys that through all time abide.

THE CHANTING CHERUBS.

WM. P. LUNT.
A. J. H.

1. Mu-sic's the lan-guage of cher-ubs in glo - ry, Chant-ing the praise of the won-der-ful Child; Tell-ing in mel-o-dy Beth-le-hem's sto - ry; Hymn-ing the tri-umphs of earth un-de-filed. Hark! on our ears breaks the many-tongued cho-rus; Min-strels ce-les-tial in vis-ion we see: Winged voic-es scat-ter the Saviour's words o'er us, "Suffer lit-tle chil-dren to come un-to me."

2. Mu-sic binds chil-dren to cher-ubs in glo - ry, Chant-ing the Bless-ed One's prais-es on high: Catch we their glad strains, re-peat we their sto - ry: Back from young lips let the wing-ed sounds fly. Sweet-est and best of the words that resound-ed From Ol-i-vet's mount or by Gal-i-lee's sea,— List! He re-peats them, by cher-ubs surround-ed, "Suffer lit-tle chil-dren to come un-to me."

SUN OF MY SOUL.

J. Keble. A. J. H.

1. Sun of my soul, Thou Saviour dear, It is not night if Thou be near. Oh, may no earth-born cloud arise To hide Thee from Thy servants eyes!
2. When the soft dews of kindly sleep My wearied eyelids gently steep, Be my last thought how sweet to rest For ever on my Saviour's breast.

3 Abide with me from morn till eve,
For without Thee I cannot live;
Abide with me when night is nigh,
For without Thee I dare not die.

4 If some poor wandering child of Thine,
Has spurn'd to-day the voice divine,
Now, Lord, the gracious work begin;
Let him no more lie down in sin.

5 Watch by the sick; enrich the poor
With blessings from Thy boundless store;
Be every mourner's sleep to-night,
Like infant slumbers, pure and light.

6 Come near and bless us when we wake,
Ere through the world our way we take,
Till in the ocean of Thy love
We lose ourselves in Heaven above.

2 The charity to bear a grief
  As if I walked alone;
 The pure, unselfish charity
  That seeketh not her own.
 The charity that would not joy
  To see another's doom.
 Would rather bear, believe, and hope,
  Or else endure the gloom.

3 The charity that will not fail
  When other things shall cease—
 And all will then be well with me
  When comes that perfect peace.
 Till then the Faith and Hope I need
  Could ne'er abide with me,
 If I should lose that loving grace,
  The "greatest of the three."

A FORM OF SERVICE

TO BE USED AT THE

OPENING OF SABBATH SCHOOL.

1. HYMN.

2. RESPONSES.

(A selection from the Psalms; the verses to be read alternately by the Superintendent and Scholars; to be followed by)

3. THE TEN COMMANDMENTS.

(To be read by the Superintendent; the Scholars to sing the response "Lord, have mercy," etc., after each commandment.)

SUPT. God spake all these words, saying, I am the Lord thy God, which have brought thee out of the land of Egypt, out of the house of bondage.

(Here the organist should play, rather softly, the music of the response, as given below, and, after a short pause)

I.

SUPT. Thou shalt have no other gods before me.

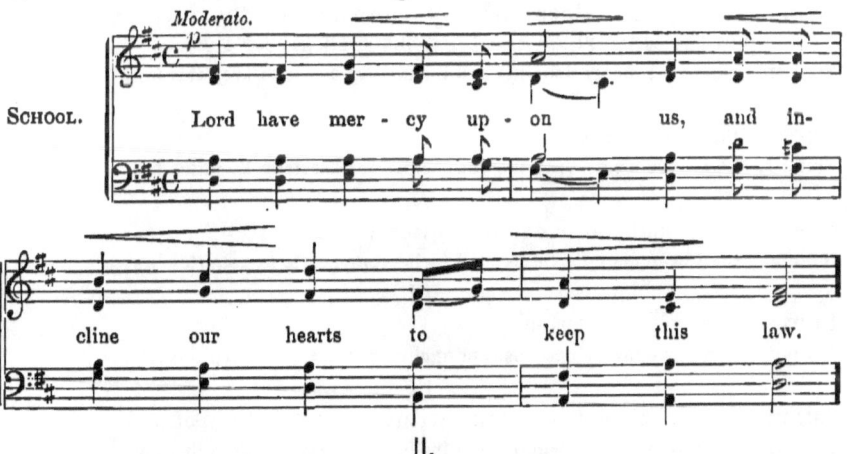

SCHOOL. Lord have mer-cy up-on us, and in-cline our hearts to keep this law.

II.

SUPT. Thou shalt not make unto thee any graven image, or any likeness of any thing that is in heaven above, or that is in the earth beneath, or that is in the water under the earth; thou shalt not bow down thyself to them, nor serve them: for I the Lord thy God am a jealous God, visiting the iniquity of the fathers upon the children unto the third and fourth generation of them that hate Me; and showing mercy unto thousands of them that love Me, and keep My commandments.

SCHOOL. Lord have mercy upon us, and incline our hearts to keep this law.

III.

SUPT. Thou shalt not take the Name of the Lord thy God in vain; for the Lord will not hold him guiltless that taketh His Name in vain.

SCHOOL. Lord have mercy upon us, and incline our hearts to keep this law.

IV.

SUPT. Remember the Sabbath-day to keep it holy. Six days shalt thou labor, and do all thy work: but the seventh day is the Sabbath of the Lord thy God; in it thou shalt not do any work, thou, nor thy son, nor thy daughter, thy man-servant, nor thy maid-servant, nor thy cattle, nor thy stranger that is within thy gates; for in six days the Lord made heaven and earth, the sea, and all that in them is, and rested, the seventh day; wherefore the Lord blessed the Sabbath-day, and hallowed it.

SCHOOL. Lord have mercy upon us, and incline our hearts to keep this law.

V.

SUPT. Honor thy father and thy mother: that thy days may be long upon the land which the Lord thy God giveth thee.

SCHOOL. Lord have mercy upon us, and incline our hearts to keep this law.

VI.

SUPT. Thou shalt not kill.

SCHOOL. Lord have mercy upon us, and incline our hearts to keep this law.

VII.

SUPT. Thou shalt not commit adultery.

SCHOOL. Lord have mercy upon us, and incline our hearts to keep this law.

VIII.

SUPT. Thou shalt not steal.

SCHOOL. Lord have mercy upon us, and incline our hearts to keep this law.

IX.

SUPT. Thou shalt not bear false witness against thy neighbor.

SCHOOL. Lord have mercy upon us, and incline our hearts to keep this law.

X.

SUPT. Thou shalt not covet thy neighbor's house, thou shalt not covet thy neighbor's wife, nor his man-servant, nor his maid-servant, nor his ox, nor his ass, nor any thing that is thy neighbor's.

SCHOOL. Lord have mer-cy up-on us, and write all these Thy laws in our hearts, we be-seech Thee.

SUPT. Thou shalt love the Lord thy God with all thy heart, and with all thy soul, and with all thy mind. This is the first and great commandment. And the second is like unto it, Thou shalt love thy neighbor as thyself. On these two commandments hang all the law and the prophets. Let us pray:

4. PRAYER.
(By the superintendent, to be followed by the)

5. LORD'S PRAYER.
(Repeated, or sung, by the entire school.)

Our Fa-ther, who art in heaven, hal-low-ed be Thy name, . . Thy king-dom come, Thy will be done on earth as it is in heaven.

(At the conclusion of the Lord's prayer, the superintendent will announce, and read a)

6. SCRIPTURE
(Selection, either from the New Testament, or the lesson for the day, after which the Opening services may conclude by singing a)

7. HYMN.

INDEX.

	PAGE
ABIDE with me, fast falls the eventide (1st Tune)	54
Abide with me, " " (2d Tune)	90
Above the clear blue sky	72
Alleluia! Alleluia!	21
All hail the power of Jesus' name	47
All hail to the day when our fathers arose	38
Am I a soldier of the cross	51
Angels from the realms of glory	9
Angels of Jesus	69
Angels roll the rock away	23
Angel voices ever singing	125
Anniversary Hymn	110
Approach not the altar with gloom in thy soul	45
Arise and bless the Lord	47
Arise, arise, ye Christians	42
A song of Thanksgiving	45
As pants the hart for cooling streams	117
At Thy feet, O Lord, we bow	59
Author of faith, to Thee, we cry	123
A voice from the desert comes awful and shrill	19
Awake, my soul, stretch every nerve	15
BANNOCKBURN	112
Beautiful Spring, bright and gay	92
Bell and prayer, song and word	18
Be Thou, O God, exalted high	137
Blessed are the pure in heart	93
Blest be the tie that binds	67
Blest day of God, most calm, most bright	61
Blest hour when mortal man retires	113
Break forth, oh earth, in joyful praise	131
Brightest and best of the sons of the morning	15
Brightly gleams our banner	108
CALM on the listening ear of night	9
Children of the heavenly King	61
Children sing, for your King	20
Christ is risen	21
Christmas Hymns:	
Angels of Bethlehem	7
Bell and prayer, song and word	18
Hark, hark, with harps of gold	10
Hark, the angels singing	41
Hark, the herald angels sing	16
Hark, the hosts of Heaven are singing	8
Hark, what mean those holy voices	7
It came upon the midnight clear	14
No more sadness now, nor fasting	13
Now to our God be praise	17
Ring the bells, Christmas bells	18
Songs of praise the angels sang	12
Christ the Lord is risen to-day (No. 1.)	23
" " " " (No. 2.)	23
Come, gracious Spirit, heavenly Dove	91
Come, holy Spirit, heavenly Dove	51
Come, kingdom of our God	57
Come, let us pray	56
Come, sound His praise abroad	81
Come, Thou Almighty King	77
Come, Thou fount of every blessing	137
Come, ye faithful raise the strain	24
Come, ye thankful people, come	48
Courage	75
Creation's praise	90
Creation's sovereign Lord	86
DEAR Lord, remember me	52
EASTER Hymns:	
Alleluia! Alleluia!	21
Children sing, for your King	20
Christ is risen	21
Come, ye faithful, raise the strain	24
Hail, thou glorious Easter morning	27

	PAGE
Let the whole creation sing	32
Proclaim the wondrous story	22
The Day of resurrection	25
Lift your glad voices	28
Easter morning	26
Evening Prayer	55
Eventide	54
Ever near me	39
FATHER in heaven	62
Father, Thou who art in heaven	58
Father, whate'er of earthly bliss	31
For all thy saints, O Lord	117
Fourth of July	38
Forward be our watchword (1st Tune)	78
" " " (2d Tune)	80
From all that dwell below the skies	67
GIFTS for Jesus	34
Give me sweet charity, my God	146
Give me thy heart, my child, while youth	120
Gleanings from the year	33
Glorious things of Thee are spoken	111
Glory to Thee, my God, this night	137
God bless our native land	37
God is Love, His mercy brightens	116
God is my strong salvation	130
God moves in a mysterious way	67
God who dwellest everywhere	112
Go when the morning shineth	53
Gracious Saviour, gentle Shepherd	139
Gracious Spirit,—Love Divine	71
Great God! beneath whose piercing eye	87
Great God! we sing that mighty hand	43
Guide me, oh Thou Great Jehovah	71
HAIL the day that sees him rise	23
Hail, thou glorious Easter morning	27
Hail to the Lord's Anointed	70
Happy soul, that, safe from harm	74
Hark, hark, my soul	69
Hark, hark, with harps of gold	10
Hark, the angels singing	41
Hark, the glad sound, the Saviour comes	9
Hark, the herald angels sing	16
Hark, the hosts of heaven are singing	8
Hark, what celestial notes	19
Hark, what mean those holy voices	7
Harvest Thanksgiving	46
Heavenly Father, as we gather	110
He hath made all things beautiful	135
He leadeth me	122
He will come, perhaps, at morning	105
Holy and reverend is the name	71
Holy Bible, Book Divine	76
Holy Spirit, Truth Divine	91
How firm a foundation	65
How gracious the promise, how soothing the word	145
How many things still dear to-day	107
How sweetly flowed the Gospel's sound	81
I HEARD the voice of Jesus say	128
I know no life divided	97
I know not where, beneath, above	134
In heavenly love abiding	94
In our work and in our play	89
In the cross of Christ I glory	142
I sing the almighty power of God	43
It came upon the midnight clear	14
JERUSALEM, the golden	114
Jesus, can a child like me	98
Jesus Christ, our Saviour	118

(151)

INDEX.

	PAGE
Jesus, give thy servants	40
Jesus, lover of my soul	123
Jesus, our Comforter	40
Jesus shall reign where'er the sun	61
Jesus, the gift divine I know	87
Jesus, we love to meet	56
Joy to the world, the Lord is come	15
LEAD, kindly light	119
Let the whole Creation sing	32
Lift your glad voices in triumph on high	28
Light of life, seraphic fire	51
Little Temples	98
Lord, dismiss us with Thy blessing	67
Lord, God Omnipotent	30
Lord, in Thy garden agony	37
Lord's Prayer (No. 1)	60
Lord's Prayer (No. 2)	62
" " (No. 3)	119
Loud raise your notes of joy	35
Love Divine, all love excelling	102
MY country, 'tis of thee	37
My faith looks up to Thee	140
My Shepherd	122
My soul, be on thy guard	43
Music's the language of cherubs in glory	143
NEARER, my God, to Thee	97
Near me, ever near me	39
No more sadness now, nor fasting	13
No, not despairingly	77
Now be the Gospel banner	129
Now God be with us	55
Now to our God be praise	17
OH, come from the land of light, sweet dove	68
Oh, come, loud anthems let us sing	87
Oh, could I speak the matchless worth	43
Oh, glad and blessed morning	26
O God, Thou art my God alone	109
O God, we praise Thee and confess	127
Oh, happy soul that lives on high	127
Oh, help us, Lord, each hour of need	103
Oh, how bright the path to heaven	135
Oh, let him whose sorrow	101
Oh, let your mingling voices rise	19
O Paradise, O Paradise (No. 1)	63
" " " " (No. 2)	73
Oh, Thou from whom all goodness flows	52
Oh, worship the King, all glorious above	81
O Zion, tune thy voice	102
Onward, Christian Soldiers	11
Onward speed thy conquering flight	95
Opening service	147
Open, Lord, my inward ear	57
Our Father in heaven	60
Our Father who art in heaven	119
Our Lord is risen from the dead	31
PALM Sunday	30
Praise to Jesus, Lord and God	96
Praise to Thee, Thou great Creator	132
Prayer (at Thy feet, O Lord, we bow)	50
Prayer of the Sabbath-school children	58
Pray without ceasing	53
Processional Hymns:—	
(Brightly gleams our banner)	108
(Forward be our watchword,—1st Tune)	78
(Forward be our watchword,—2d Tune)	80
(Onward, Christian Soldiers)	11
(We march, we march,—1st Tune)	82
(We march, we march,—2d Tune)	84
Proclaim the wondrous story	22
REJOICE! the Lord is King	44
Resting in faith	74
Ride on, ride on, in majesty	37
Ring the Bells, Christmas Bells	18

	PAGE
Rise my soul and stretch thy wings	57
Rock of Ages, cleft for me	113
SABBATH Bells	65
Sadly bend the flowers	58
Safely through another week	47
Saviour, blessed Saviour	124
Saviour, breathe an evening blessing	113
Shine out, sun, more bright than ever	33
Softly, now, the light of day	123
Sometimes a light surprises	115
Songs of praise the angels sang	12
Stand up and bless the Lord	61
Stand up! stand up, for Jesus	85
"Suffer the little children to come unto me"	107
Sun of my soul, Thou Saviour dear	144
Suppliant, lo! Thy children bend	79
Sweet charity	146
Sweet hour of prayer	109
THANKSGIVING Day	50
Thanks be to God	50
Thanksgiving Hymn (Come, ye thankful people, come)	48
Thanksgiving Hymn (Rejoice! the Lord is King)	44
The angels of Bethlehem	7
The beauty of youthful holiness	100
The birds that speed their fearless flight	116
The chanting cherubs	143
The Christian soldier	85
The coming of the Lord	105
The Day of Resurrection	25
The Father's call	120
The gathering place	134
The Gospel Banner	129
The heavens declare His glory	136
The heavens declare Thy glory, Lord	77
The Holy Dove	68
The Lord is my Shepherd	121
The Lord my pasture shall prepare	127
The nation's prayer	139
The ninety-and-nine	6
There were ninety-and-nine	6
The thing my God doth hate	3
The triumph of Christ	21
The wild-bird's lesson	16
They who seek the throne of grace	117
Though faint, yet pursuing, we go on our way	91
Thou whose wide, extended sway	112
Through the night of doubt and sorrow	75
Thy presence, gracious God afford	81
'Tis by the faith of joys to come	31
To Thee, my God and Saviour	141
Triumph of Christ	131
Trust in God	101
WAIT on the Lord	106
Walk in the light; so shalt thou know	87
We bring no glitt'ring treasure	133
We come in childhood's innocence	138
Welcome, delightful morn	71
Welcome, sweet day of rest	117
We march, we march, to victory (1st Tune)	82
" " " " " (2d Tune)	84
We never part from Thee	112
We plough the fields and scatter	46
We sing thy mighty power of God	49
What a Friend we have in Jesus	76
Whatever is best and completest	34
When clouds hang heavy o'er thy way	106
When His salvation bringing	104
When in shadow dark, a flower	100
When Israel, of the Lord beloved	137
When o'er the world awaking	66
When shall the voice of singing	126
While Thee I seek, protecting Power	109
While with ceaseless course, the sun	31
Who, my humble beast bestriding	30
Wide as His vast dominion lies	51
YE realms below the skies	99

www.ingramcontent.com/pod-product-compliance
Lightning Source LLC
Chambersburg PA
CBHW030340170426
43202CB00010B/1186